COLLINS ILLUSTRATED FIRST DICTIONARY

This edition published 1997 for Remainders Ltd
by Diamond Books
77 - 85 Fulham Palace Road
Hammersmith, London W6 8JB

First published in 1989 in the United Kingdom
by William Collins Sons & Co. Ltd as *Collins First Dictionary*

ISBN 0 26166 959 1

Printed by Rotolito Lombarda, Italy

COLLINS ILLUSTRATED FIRST DICTIONARY

Written by Evelyn Goldsmith

Illustrated by Penny Dann

Consultant editor Ginny Lapage

Introduction

This dictionary is for young readers of seven and upwards. The right level of vocabulary for the age group has been chosen on the advice of experienced teachers and librarians. We have included words which children already know or have nearly mastered, and those they can be expected to meet in reading, learning and conversation.

The definitions are remarkable in that a full sentence is used to explain each word. This not only makes the meaning more accessible: it also shows how the word itself is used in context. So for instance the entry for **abroad** reads "When you go abroad, you go to a different country." If extra help seems to be needed where words are more difficult to define, a sentence is given as an example.

Other features include the comparative and superlative forms of adjectives: for example, **bad** (worse, worst); and in the case of some nouns added information such as the part of the world an animal comes from, or what a particular material might be used for.

All the definitions have been field tested with children of the appropriate age group, and adjusted where necessary.

The large format, clear typography and specially drawn illustrations combine to give a lively, friendly feel to the whole dictionary. We hope that it will give many hours of enjoyment as well as providing a valuable source of reference.

How to use this dictionary

You can use a dictionary for lots of things. You can find out what a word means. You can see that sometimes a word has more than one meaning. If you are not quite sure how to spell something, the dictionary can help. And it can also show you how to use a word properly.

You will find it easy to look up words in your dictionary if you can say the letters of the alphabet in the right order: **a b c** and so on, right through to **z**. If you are not sure of the order that all the letters go in, the alphabet is printed at the bottom of this page so that you can check it.

Suppose you want to look up **butterfly**. It begins with **b**. Turn the pages until you come to the words beginning with **b**. There are lots of **b** words. How can you find **butterfly** without looking at every one? Look at the second letter of **butterfly**. It is **u**. Keep looking down the columns until you come to the words beginning with **bu**. Now you can see there are lots of words beginning with **bu**. Where can **butterfly** be? Look at the third letter of **butterfly**. It is a **t**. Keep looking until you come to words beginning with **but**, now **butterfly** really cannot be far away. There it is, just under **buttercup**. The dictionary sometimes shows you a picture of the word as well as telling you about it. You will see that **butterfly** has a picture above the word.

As you get used to looking up words in the dictionary, you will find you can do it much more quickly!

ability If you have the ability to do something, you can do it.

abroad When you go abroad, you go to a different country.

absent If someone is absent, they are not here.

accident
1 An accident is something nasty that happens by chance: *He broke his leg in a climbing accident.*
2 If something happens by accident, it has not been planned: *They were pleased when they met by accident in the supermarket.*

ache (say ake) An ache is a dull, lasting pain.

acorn An acorn is a nut which grows on an oak tree. You cannot eat acorns, but if you plant one an oak tree may begin to grow.

act
1 When you act you do something: *He had to act quickly to put the fire out.*
2 If you take part in a play you are acting.
3 An act is something you do: *It was a brave act to rescue the man from the sea.*
4 Stage plays are divided into parts called acts.

active Someone who is active moves about a lot, or is very busy

address Your address is the name or number of your house, and the street and town where you live.

admire
1 When you admire somebody, you think very highly of them.
2 When you admire something, you enjoy looking at it: *They stopped the car to admire the view.*

adult An adult is a grown-up person or animal.

adventure If you are having an adventure, you are doing something exciting and perhaps even dangerous.

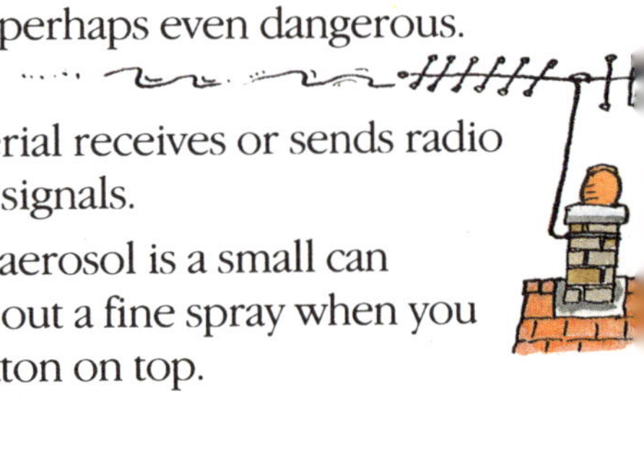

aerial An aerial receives or sends radio or television signals.

aerosol An aerosol is a small can which sends out a fine spray when you press the button on top.

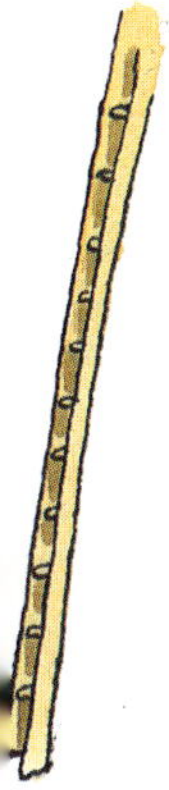

affection is a feeling of fondness for somebody: *He thought of his grandmother with great affection.*

afford If you can afford something, you have enough money to buy it, or to do it: *They decided they could afford to go on a camping holiday.*

afraid Someone who is afraid thinks something nasty might happen: *He was afraid to climb the ladder in case he fell.*

afternoon The afternoon is part of the day. It starts at 12 o'clock and ends at about 6 o'clock.

again If you do something again, you do it once more.

age
1 Your age is the number of years you have lived.
2 An age is a special period in history, like the Stone Age.

ago If something happened four days ago, it is four days since it happened.

aim If you aim at something, you point a weapon at it.

air
1 Air is the mixture of gases that we breathe.
2 If you go by air, you fly in an aircraft.

aircraft An aircraft is any vehicle which flies. Helicopters, gliders and aeroplanes are all aircraft.

alarm
1 Alarm is a feeling of fear: *He looked at the bear with great alarm.*
2 An alarm is something like a bell or flashing light that warns you of something.

album An album is a special book with blank pages that you can fill with things like stamps or photographs.

alive If a person or animal is alive, they are living now.

all
1 You say all when you mean the whole of something: *Give her all of it, I don't want any.*
2 You can also say all when you mean everybody or everything: *All the children helped, and soon all the toys were cleared away.*

alligator An alligator is a reptile. It is of the same family as a crocodile, but smaller. An American alligator is about 3 metres long. The female lays from 20 to 70 eggs in a large nest made of mud.

allow If someone allows you to do something, they let you do it.

almost means very nearly, but not quite: *He tripped and almost fell.*

alone If you are alone there is nobody with you.

aloud If you read something aloud, you read so that people can hear you.

alphabet An alphabet is all the letters used to write words in a language. The letters of an alphabet are written in a special order.

already If you have done something already, you did it earlier: *I've already done the washing up.*

alter When you alter something, you change it in some way.

always
1 If you always do something, you do it every time: *He always puts his toys away when he has finished playing.*
2 If something has always been so, it has been that way for as long as anybody can remember: *They have always been good friends.*
3 If you say you will do something always, you mean you will keep on doing it: *I shall always love you.*

ambulance An ambulance is a vehicle that is used to take people to hospital.

amount An amount is how much you have or need of something: *When my brother comes we eat twice the usual amount.*

amuse If you amuse somebody, you make them smile, or stop them feeling bored.

ancient (say ainshent)
1 If something is ancient it is very old.
2 Ancient history is about things that happened a very long time ago.

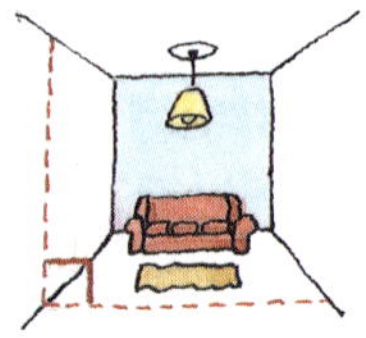

angle An angle is the shape that is made when two lines or surfaces join.

angry (angrier, angriest) If you feel angry you are very cross.

animal All living things except plants are animals. Human beings, cats, dogs, birds, fish, reptiles, and insects are all animals.

ankle Your ankle is the joint between your foot and your leg.

annoy If you annoy somebody you make them cross.

annual
1 Annual means something that happens once a year, like a birthday or school sports day.
2 An annual is a book that comes out once a year.

answer
1 If someone asks you something, whatever you say next is your answer.
2 When you answer the telephone, you pick it up when it rings.

ant Ants are small insects which live in large groups called colonies. There are more than 5000 different kinds of ant.

antelope Antelopes are animals that look like deer, but with horns instead of antlers. They live in Africa and Asia. .

ape Apes are like monkeys but are larger and have no tails. Chimpanzees, gorillas, gibbons and orang-outangs are all apes.

appearance
1 Your appearance is the way you look to other people: *I wish you would do more about your appearance and comb your hair.*
2 If someone makes an appearance they arrive suddenly.

appetite If you have an appetite you are looking forward to eating something.

apple An apple is a crisp round fruit which grows on a tree.

apricot An apricot is a small round yellow-orange fruit with a large stone in the centre. It grows on trees in parts of Asia, Europe and the United States.

April is the fourth month of the year. It has 30 days.

aquarium An aquarium is a glass tank filled with water. You can keep fish and other underwater animals in it.

arch An arch is usually made from brick, stone or iron, in the shape of a curve. It is used to span openings such as doorways, or between pillars on bridges.

area
1 The area of something flat is its size.
2 If you want to talk about things in or around a place, you use the word area: *There are lots of shops in the city area.*

argue If you argue with somebody, you show that you do not agree with them, and give your reasons.

arithmetic is about adding, subtracting, multiplying and dividing numbers.

arm
1 Your arm is the part of your body between the shoulder and the hand.
2 If you arm somebody, you give them a weapon.

army An army is a large organized group of people who are armed and trained to fight on land in case of war.

arrange
1 If you arrange something like a party or a holiday, you make plans for it.
2 If you arrange things like books or flowers, you group them in a special way.

arrive
1 When you arrive at a place, you reach it at the end of your journey.
2 When something like a letter or a newspaper arrives, it is delivered to you.

arrow
1 An arrow is a long thin weapon which is shot from a bow. It has a point at one end, and usually feathers at the other.
2 An arrow can be a sign which shows people which way to go.

art is something like painting or sculpture which is beautiful or has a special meaning.

ash
1 Ash is the dust that is left over from a fire.
2 An ash is a tree. It can grow to about 35 metres.

ask
1 When you ask somebody something, you are trying to find something out.
2 If you ask somebody for something, you hope they will give it to you.

asleep If you are asleep your eyes are closed and your whole body is resting.

astonish If you astonish somebody, you surprise them very much.

astronaut An astronaut is somebody who is trained to fly in a spacecraft.

atlas An atlas is a book of maps.

atmosphere The Earth's atmosphere is the air around it.

attack If a person attacks somebody they try to hurt them.

attic An attic is a room at the top of a house, just under the roof.

attractive
1 If something is attractive it is nice to look at.
2 If you are attractive people want to be near you.

audience An audience is a group of people watching or listening to something like a play, film, talk or piece of music.

August is the eighth month of the year. It has thirty-one days.

autumn is the season between summer and winter.

avalanche An avalanche is a great amount of snow and ice that falls down a mountain.

avenue An avenue is a wide road with trees on either side.

awake If you are awake you are not sleeping.

awful If you say something is awful you mean it is very bad: *The weather was so awful we couldn't go out.*

awkward
1 If people are awkward, or behave awkwardly, they are clumsy and do not move gracefully.
2 If you say someone can be awkward to deal with, you mean they might not be very helpful or nice.

axe An axe is a tool with a long handle and a heavy sharp blade at one end. It is used for chopping wood.

baby A baby is a very young child.

back Your back is the part of your body which is behind you, from your neck to the top of your legs.

bacon is meat which comes from the back or sides of a pig and has been salted and sometimes smoked.

bad (worse, worst)
1 You say bad when you are talking about somebody who is naughty or wicked.
2 Bad food is not fresh.
3 Bad work is work that has not been well done.

badge People sometimes wear badges to let you know they belong to a school or a club. Cars have badges to let you know what make they are.

bag A bag is for carrying or holding things. It is soft, and usually made of paper, cloth, or plastic.

bait is food that you use to trap animals: *I put a worm on the hook as bait.*

bake When you bake food, you cook it in the oven.

baker A baker makes and sells bread, cakes and pies. The place where a baker works is called a bakery.

balance: When you balance you keep steady: *He tried to balance on one leg.*

balcony A balcony is a platform fixed to the outside of a building with a railing or wall around it.

bald (balder, baldest) People who are bald have no hair on the top of their head.

ball You need a ball for lots of games, like tennis and football. Each game needs a different sort of ball.

balloon A balloon is a small rubber bag. If you blow hard into it, it gets bigger and makes a very light toy or decoration.

bamboo is a kind of grass which often grows much higher than a person. It has strong hollow stems which are useful for garden canes or for making furniture.

banana A banana is a fruit which grows on trees in hot countries. Bananas hang from the tree in bunches of about a hundred.

band
1 A band is a small number of people, like a band of robbers or a group of musicians.
2 A band can also mean a strip of material such as iron, cloth or rubber.

bandage
1 A bandage is a strip of cloth used to cover a wound or tie up an injury.
2 To bandage someone you wind a strip of clean cloth round the part that is injured.

bandit A bandit is a robber who steals from travellers.

banister A banister is one of the posts that hold up a handrail on stairs.

bank
1 A bank is a building which has strong rooms for keeping people's money safe.
2 The bank of a river is the ground either side of the water.

bare (barer, barest)
1 If a part of your body is bare, it is not covered by clothes.
2 If a room is bare, it has no furniture in it.

bark
1 A bark is a loud noise that dogs make.
2 Bark is the outside covering of a tree.

barn A barn is a large building where a farmer stores hay and other crops.

barrel
1 A barrel is a wooden, metal or plastic container.
2 The barrel is the long metal part of a gun.

base The base is the bottom of something.

basket A basket is usually made from strips of thin wood or cane, and is used for holding or carrying things.

bat
1 In some games such as table-tennis or baseball you need a bat to hit the ball.
2 A bat is a small animal like a mouse with leathery wings. It flies at night, and sleeps hanging upside down.

bath A bath is a container for water. It is big enough to sit or lie in, so that you can wash yourself all over.

bathroom The bathroom is where the bath or shower is.

battery A battery is a thing which gives you electric power. You use tiny batteries for things like watches, and large batteries for cars and other vehicles.

battle A battle is a fight between enemy forces, on land, at sea, or in the air.

beach The beach is the place full of sand and pebbles that is close to the sea.

bead A bead is a small piece of something like coloured glass or plastic with a hole through it.

beak A beak is the hard outside part of a bird's mouth that it uses for picking up food.

bean A bean is a vegetable. Its outer covering is called a pod, and inside it has several large seeds. The seeds are also called beans.

bear A bear is a large heavy animal measuring up to three metres. It usually makes its home in a cave.

beard A beard is hair which grows on the lower part of a man's face.

beautiful
1 You say something is beautiful if it gives you great pleasure to look at it or listen to it.
2 You say somebody is beautiful if you think they are lovely to look at.

beaver A beaver is a thickset animal, nearly a metre long. It has a flat scaly tail and webbed back feet. A beaver's home is called a lodge, built from sticks plastered with mud.

bed
1 A bed is something to lie down on when you rest or sleep.
2 The bed of a sea or river is the bottom of it.

bedroom The bedroom is the room where you sleep.

bee A bee is a flying insect. Bees are important to flowers and fruit trees, and some people keep them for the honey and wax that they make. (See swarm).

beef is the meat from a bull or a cow.

beehive A beehive is a house for bees made so that the beekeeper can collect the honey.

beetle A beetle is an insect with four wings. The front two act as hard covers to the body when the beetle is not flying.

begin
1 When you begin, you start to do something.
2 When something begins, it starts at that time: *School begins on Thursday.*

behave
1 If someone is behaving badly, they are not being good.
2 If someone tells you to behave yourself, they want you to be good.

believe If you believe somebody or something, you think what is being said is true.

bell A bell is a piece of metal shaped like a cup which rings when something hits it.

belong
1 If something belongs to you, it is your own.
2 If you belong to something like a club, you are a member of it.
3 If something belongs to something else, it is part of it, or fits it: *I think this piece belongs to that jigsaw.*

belt
1 A belt is a strip of material such as leather or plastic that you put round your waist.
2 A seat belt is fixed inside a vehicle like a car or an aeroplane.

bench
1 A bench is a long seat, usually made of wood.
2 In a workshop or laboratory a bench is a table where people work.

bend When something bends, it becomes curved or crooked.

berry A berry is a small round soft fruit that grows on a bush or a tree. Some berries are good to eat, but others are poisonous.

beware You tell people to beware if there is danger of some kind.

bicycle A bicycle is a vehicle with two wheels. You sit on it and turn pedals with your feet to make it go.

big (bigger, biggest)
1 Something or somebody big is large in size.
2 If you have a big brother or sister they are older than you are.

bird A bird is an animal with feathers. It has two legs and two wings. Most birds can fly. The young are hatched from eggs.

birth The birth of a baby is when it comes out of its mother's body.

birthday Your birthday is a special date that is remembered every year, because it was the day you were born.

biscuit A biscuit is a small flat crisp kind of cake.

bit
1 A bit of something is a small piece of it: *You've got a bit of jam on your face.*
2 A bit is a piece of metal that goes in a horse's mouth when you put the reins on.

bite If you bite something you cut it with your teeth.

blackberry A blackberry is a small soft dark purple fruit that grows wild.

blackbird A blackbird is about 25 cm long. The male has black feathers and a yellow beak. The female has brown feathers.

blackcurrant Blackcurrants are very small dark purple fruit. They grow in bunches on bushes.

blade
1 The blade of something which cuts, like a knife, is the thin flat piece with a sharp edge.
2 A single piece of grass is called a blade.

blame If somebody blames a person for something bad that happened, they think or say that person made it happen.

blanket A blanket is a large warm cloth, often used to cover people in bed.

blast-off is the moment a rocket leaves the ground to begin its journey into space.

blaze A blaze is a strong, bright fire.

bleed If a part of you bleeds, you lose blood.

blind
1 A blind is rolled material that you pull down to cover a window.
2 Someone who is blind cannot see because of something wrong with their eyes.

blindfold A blindfold is a piece of cloth to tie around a person's head and cover their eyes so that they cannot see.

blizzard A blizzard is a very bad snowstorm with strong winds.

block
1 A block is a large piece of something like wood or stone, with straight or nearly straight sides.
2 A block of flats is a tall building with lots of rooms where people live.
3 If something blocks your way, you cannot get past.

blood is the red liquid that your heart pumps round inside your body.

blot A blot is a mark usually made by spilling a drop of ink.

blouse A blouse is a piece of clothing made of light material, which girls or women sometimes wear on the top half of their body.

blow
1 When the wind blows, the air moves.
2 When you blow you send air out of your mouth.
3 A blow is when someone is hit very hard.

blunt (blunter, bluntest) If a knife is blunt it does not cut properly.

board
1 A board is a flat piece of something like wood.
2 If you board a ship, train or aircraft you get on it to go somewhere.

boat A boat is a small vessel for travelling on water. It can hold only a few people.

body A person's or animal's body is every part of them.

boil
1 When liquid boils it gets very hot. It starts bubbling, and steam rises from it.
2 A boil is a painful red swelling on the skin.

bone A person's or animal's bones are the hard parts inside their body which make up the skeleton.

bonfire A bonfire is a fire that is lit outdoors, usually to burn garden rubbish.

book A book is pieces of paper fixed together on one edge, inside a cover, with a story or ideas written inside.

boot
1 A boot is a shoe that covers the whole foot and part of the leg.
2 The boot of a car is the space for luggage.

bore
1 If you bore a hole in something, you make a hole with a tool like a drill.
2 If somebody bores you, you find them uninteresting, and you begin to feel tired and impatient.

born When a baby is born, it comes out of its mother's body and begins its life as a separate person.

borrow When you borrow something, somebody lets you have it for a while, but they expect you to give it back later: *May I borrow your pencil for ten minutes please?*

bottle A bottle is a container for keeping liquids in. Bottles are usually made of glass or plastic.

bottom The bottom of anything is its lowest part: *She looked up from the bottom of the steps.*

bounce When something bounces, it springs back in the opposite direction as soon as it hits something hard, like the ground or a wall.

bow (as in so)
1 A bow is a kind of knot with two loops used to tie laces and ribbons.

2 A bow is also a weapon used for shooting arrows.
3 The bow of a stringed musical instrument is a long piece of wood with horsehair stretched along it.

bow (as in now) When you bow, you stand in front of someone and bend your body forward.

bowl A bowl is a container with an open top. Bowls are usually round and not very deep.

box A box is a container with straight sides, made from something stiff like cardboard, wood or plastic.

boy A boy is a male child.

bracelet A bracelet is a band or chain, usually made of metal. You wear it round your wrist or arm as an ornament.

brake The brake is the part of any vehicle or machine that slows it down or stops it.

branch A branch is a part of a tree that grows out from the trunk.

brass is a yellow-coloured metal made from a mixture of copper and zinc. It can be used for making ornaments and some musical instruments.

brave (braver, bravest) If you are brave you show that you can do something even if it is frightening.

bread is a very common food made with flour and baked in an oven.

break If you break something it splits into pieces, or stops working.

breakfast is the first meal of the day.

breath Your breath is the air that you take into and let out of your lungs: *Take a deep breath before you go under the water.*

breathe When you breathe you take air into your lungs through your nose or mouth, and then let it out again.

breeze A breeze is a gentle wind.

brick A brick is a block used for building. It is made of baked clay.

bride A bride is a woman on or near her wedding day.

bridegroom A bridegroom is a man on or near his wedding day.

bridesmaid A bridesmaid is a woman or a girl who helps the bride on her wedding day.

bridge A bridge is something built over things like rivers, railways or roads, so that people or vehicles can get across.

brief (briefer, briefest) If something is brief it does not last very long: *His answer was very brief - he just said "No".*

bright (brighter, brightest)
1 Bright colours or lights are clear and easy to see.
2 Someone who is bright is quick at learning or noticing things.

brim
1 The brim of a hat is the lower part of it that sticks out from the head.
2 If you fill a cup to the brim with liquid, you fill it right up to the top.

bring
1 If you bring someone on a visit, they come with you.
2 If you bring something you have it with you when you arrive.
3 If you bring something to an end, you stop it.

brittle (brittler, brittlest) If something is brittle, it is hard but easily broken.

broad (broader, broadest) Something such as a road or a river that is broad is very wide.

broadcast A broadcast is something you hear on radio or see on television.

brooch (say broach) A brooch is a small piece of jewellery with a pin on the back of it.

brook A brook is a small natural stream of fast moving fresh water.

broom A broom is a kind of brush with a long handle. You can use a broom to sweep the floor or other places where you walk.

bruise A bruise is an injury, usually made when part of the body is hit by something. The skin is not broken, but a purple mark appears.

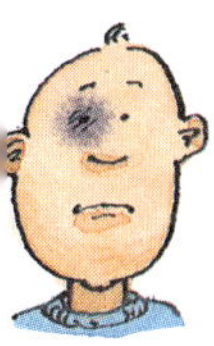

brush
1 A brush is a lot of bristles, fixed into wood, metal or plastic.
2 If you brush against something, you touch it lightly as you are passing.

bubble
1 A bubble is a hollow, very light ball of soap or liquid.
2 When a liquid bubbles, it makes a lot of bubbles because it is boiling or fizzy.

bucket A bucket is a container with an open top and a handle. It is often used for carrying water.

buckle A buckle is a fastening which is fixed to one end of a belt or strap.

bud A bud is a small lump on a plant that will open into a leaf or flower.

build If you build something, you make it by joining things together.

building A building is something like a house or a factory that has walls and a roof.

bulb
1 A bulb is the part of an electric lamp that is made of glass.
2 A bulb is also a root shaped like an onion. Many spring flowers such as daffodils and tulips grow from bulbs.

bull A bull is a male animal of the cattle family.

bulldozer A bulldozer is a large, powerful tractor with a steel blade on the front. It is used for moving large amounts of earth or stone.

bullet A bullet is a small piece of metal with a rounded end that is fired from a gun.

bump
1 If you bump into something, you hit it while you are moving.
2 A bump is a small swelling that comes up when something has hit you.

bunch
1 A bunch of flowers is a number of flowers on their stems which have been picked and put together.
2 A bunch of fruit is a group growing together on one stem. Bananas and grapes grow in bunches.

bundle A bundle is a number of small things that have been tied together so that they can be carried or stored.

bungalow A bungalow is a house with all its rooms on one floor.

bunk beds are two single beds fixed one above the other.

burn
1 A burn is an injury caused by heat or fire.
2 If something is burning, it is being spoiled or destroyed by fire.
3 People often burn fuel, such as coal, to keep warm.

burrow A burrow is a hole in the ground or a tunnel dug by a small animal such as a rabbit, to live in or to take shelter.

bury
1 When you bury something, you put it in a hole in the ground and cover it up.
2 When you bury your face in something, you hide or partly hide your face in it.

bus A bus is a large vehicle which travels on the road, stopping at bus stops. People pay to go on buses.

bush
1 A bush is a large woody plant with lots of branches. It is smaller than a tree.
2 The bush is the wild area of Australia, New Zealand, and Africa.

busy
1 When you are busy, you are working hard on something, or giving it your full attention.
2 A place that is busy is full of people doing things or moving about.

butter is a solid yellowish fat which is made from cream. You can spread it on bread or use it for cooking.

buttercup A buttercup is a small bright yellow wild flower.

butterfly A butterfly is an insect with four large wings. Butterflies' babies are caterpillars, which hatch from eggs. When the caterpillars are ready, they spin a cocoon round themselves, and later come out as a butterfly.

button
1 A button is a small round fastening sewn on to clothes such as shirts.
2 A button is also a small part of something electrical that you press to make it work.

buy When you buy something, you get it by paying money for it.

cab
1 The cab is the place where the driver sits in a bus, truck or train.
2 A cab is a taxi.

cabbage A cabbage is a vegetable that looks like a large ball of leaves. The leaves can be green, white or purple.

cabin
1 A cabin is a room in a ship, boat or aeroplane for passengers or crew.
2 A cabin is also a small house, usually made of wood, in a wild place such as a forest.

cactus A cactus is a thick fleshy plant. It is covered with spikes and has no leaves.

café A café is a place where there are tables and chairs and you can buy drinks and snacks.

cage A cage is a box or room made with bars. Pets like birds, hamsters and gerbils are usually kept in cages, and some of the animals in zoos also live in cages.

cake A cake is a sweet food made with flour, sugar, fat and eggs, and baked in the oven.

calculator A calculator is something which gives you the answer to sums if you press the right buttons.

calendar A calendar is a chart which divides the year into months, weeks and days.

call
1 If you call somebody something, you give them a name
2 If you call somebody, you shout for them, or telephone them.
3 If you call on somebody, you go to see them for a little while.

calm
1 If you are calm, you do not seem worried or excited.
2 If a lake or the sea is calm, it is, smooth and still because there is no wind.

camel A camel is a large animal which carries people and things in the desert. There are two kinds of camel. The Arabian camel has one hump, and the Bactrian camel has two.

camera A camera is something you use to take photographs.

camp A camp is a place where people live in tents.

can
1 A can is a metal container for things such as food, drink or paint.
2 You say you can do something if you are able to do it.
3 If you ask if you can do something, you want to know if you are allowed to do it.

candle A candle is a stick made of wax. It has a piece of string, called a wick, through the length of it.

cannon A cannon is a large gun, usually on wheels. They were once used to fire heavy metal balls at the enemy in battle.

canoe A canoe is a small light boat, usually pointed at both ends.

cap
1 A cap is a soft flat hat with a peak at the front.
2 A cap is also a small flat lid on a bottle or container.

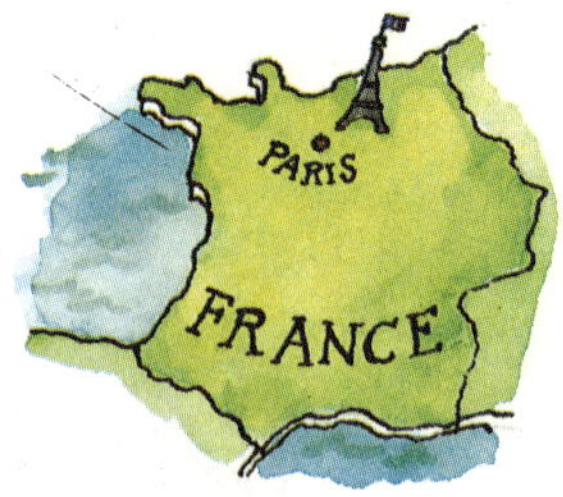

capital
1 The capital is the main city in a country: *Paris is the capital of France.*

2 A capital is a big letter of the alphabet. People's names start with a capital letter.

capture If you capture somebody you take them prisoner.

car A car is a road vehicle powered by an engine.

caravan A caravan is a vehicle with beds and a place to cook, so that people can spend holidays or live in it. Some caravans can be pulled along the road by a car.

card
1 Card is strong stiff paper.
2 Playing cards are small pieces of card with numbers or pictures on them. They are used for card games.
3 A greetings card usually has a picture on the front and words inside and is sent to people on special days, such as a birthday.

cardboard is a thick stiff board made of paper. It is used to make things like boxes.

cardigan A cardigan is a knitted jacket. You fasten it at the front with buttons or a zip.

care
1 If you care about something, you think it is important.
2 If you care for somebody, you like them very much.
3 If you take care of something such as an animal, you look after it well so that it stays healthy and happy.

careful If you tell someone to be careful you want them to behave sensibly and think about what they are doing.

carnival A carnival is a special sort of party in the streets that anyone can go to. There is usually music and dancing, and people dress up and decorate cars and trucks.

carpet A carpet is a thick covering usually made of something like wool. People put carpets on floors and stairs to make them quiet and comfortable to walk on.

carriage
1 A carriage is one of the vehicles that are joined together to make up a passenger train.
2 A carriage is also an old-fashioned vehicle with four wheels, pulled by one or more horses.

carrot A carrot is a long thin orange-coloured vegetable that grows under the ground.

carry When you carry something, you hold it off the ground and take it with you.

cart A cart is a heavy wooden vehicle pulled by horses or cattle on farms.

carton
1 A carton is a strong cardboard box for packing things in.
2 A carton is a container made of cardboard or plastic to hold food or drink.

cartoon
1 A cartoon is a funny drawing in a magazine or newspaper.
2 A cartoon film is a film where the actors are drawn instead of being real.

case
1 A case is a box to keep or carry things in.
2 In museums and shops, a case is a container for displaying things.

cash is money in coins and banknotes.

castle A castle is large building with very strong walls.

cat A cat is a small mammal. Domestic cats are kept as pets. There are also larger cats, such as lions and tigers.

catch
1 A catch is a fastener on a lid or a door.
2 If you catch something like a ball you take hold of it when it is moving.
3 If you catch a bus or a train, you get on it to go somewhere.
4 If you catch something like measles, you get the illness.

caterpillar A caterpillar is a small animal like a worm with legs, that will turn into a butterfly or moth.

cathedral A cathedral is the main church in a large area.

cattle Bulls and cows on the farm are called cattle.

cauliflower A cauliflower is a vegetable. It has a large white centre, and leaves round the outside.

cave A cave is a large hole in the side of a cliff or hill, or under the ground.

ceiling The ceiling is the inside roof of a room.

cellar A cellar is a room under a house. Cellars are often used for storing things in.

cement is a grey powder made from limestone and clay. When it is mixed with sand and water it makes mortar for sticking bricks together.

centimetre A centimetre is a measure of length. It is the same as 10 millimetres.

centipede A centipede is a small animal. It looks like a tiny worm, but it has a lot of legs.

centre The centre of anything is the middle of it.

century A century is one hundred years.

cereal
1 Cereal is a plant which has seeds called grain that can be used for food.
2 Cereal is also a food made from grain that is often eaten for breakfast.

certain
1 If something is known for certain, it is true.
2 If you are certain of something, you are sure it is true.

certificate A certificate is a special piece of paper which says that something important took place.

chain A chain is made from rings of metal joined together in a line.

chair A chair is a seat with a back, for one person.

chalk is a soft white rock. It can be made into sticks to write or draw.

champion A champion is someone who has beaten everyone else in a contest: *She was the champion chess player in our school last year*

chance If something happens by chance, it has not been planned.

change
1 Change is money you are given when you pay too much for something because you do not have the right amount.
2 When something changes it becomes different.
3 When you change your clothes you put on different ones.
4 When you change trains you get off one and on to another.

channel
1 A channel is a passage for water or other liquid.
2 Television companies use different channels to broadcast programmes.

chart
1 A chart is a sheet of paper showing things like dates or numbers clearly.
2 A chart can also be a map of the sea or of the stars.

chase If you chase a person or animal you run after them to try and catch them.

cheap (cheaper, cheapest) Something which is cheap costs very little money, or less than you might expect.

check
1 A check is a square pattern.
2 If you check something, you make sure it is right, or safe.

checkout A checkout is the place in a supermarket where you pay.

cheek Your cheeks are the soft parts of your face on each side of your nose and mouth.

cheerful Someone who is cheerful shows they are feeling happy.

cheese is a food made from milk. It can be hard or soft. Some cheeses have a strong flavour.

cheetah A cheetah is a large wild animal of the cat family. Cheetahs can run very fast, reaching over 100km an hour.

cherry A cherry is a small round fruit with a hard seed in the middle called a stone. Cherries can be red, yellow or black.

chess is a game for two people, played on a board marked out in squares.

chest
1 Your chest is the top part of the front of your body, between your neck and your waist.
2 A chest is a large heavy box, usually made of wood.

chew When you chew food, you bite it several times to make it easier to swallow.

chicken
1 A chicken is a bird which is kept on a farm. Most of the eggs that we eat are laid by female chickens, called hens.
2 Chicken is the meat of a chicken.

chicken-pox is a disease caught especially by children. It causes a high temperature and spots that itch.

child A child is a young boy or girl. Two or more boys or girls are called children.

chimney A chimney is a pipe which goes up from a fireplace or factory furnace to above the level of the roof. It takes the smoke up into the air.

chimpanzee A chimpanzee is an ape, smaller than a gorilla. Chimpanzees live in rain forests.

china is a fine clay mixture used to make things like cups, saucers and plates, and also ornaments.

chip
1 A chip is a long thin fried piece of potato.
2 A chip is also a small piece that has broken off something.
3 A silicon chip is a tiny piece of special material that is used in computers.

chocolate is a brown sweet or drink made from cocoa.

choir A choir is a group of people who sing together, often in a church or at school.

choke If you choke, you cannot breathe properly because there is not enough air getting to your lungs.

choose When you choose something you pick out the one you want.

chop
1 A chop is a small piece of meat on a bone.
2 When somebody chops something like wood, they cut it with an axe.

church A church is a building where people worship.

cinema A cinema is a place where people watch films.

circle A circle is a curved line with both ends joined, making the shape of a ring.

circus A circus is a group of people such as clowns, acrobats and jugglers who travel to different places to give shows.

city A city is a very large busy town.

clap When you clap, you make a noise by hitting your hands together.

classroom A classroom is a room in a school where children have lessons.

claw The claws of a bird or animal are the hard curved nails at the end of its feet.

clay is a special sort of sticky earth that goes hard when it is dry. It is used for making bricks and pots.

clean (cleaner, cleanest)
Something is clean if it is free of dirt and stains.

clear (clear, clearest)
1 If something you say is clear, it is easy to understand.
2 If a thing is clear, you can see through it.

clever
1 Someone who is clever is able to learn and understand things easily.
2 You say someone is clever if they are very skilled at something.

cliff A cliff is a hill with very steep sides that go almost straight down. You often find cliffs near the sea.

climate The climate of a place is the sort of weather it usually has.

climb When you climb something like a mountain or a tree, you move towards the top of it. Climbing is usually quite hard work.

clinic A clinic is where people go to see doctors or to get help and advice about their health.

clip A clip is something small and springy which holds things in place.

cloak A cloak is a loose coat that fastens at the neck, and does not have any sleeves.

clock A clock is an instrument that measures time, and shows you what the time is. Clocks with numbers instead of hands are called digital clocks.

clothes are the things people wear, such as shirts, trousers and dresses.

cloud
1 A cloud is a patch of white or grey mist that floats in the sky.
2 You can say cloud to describe a lot of smoke, steam or dust.

club A club is a group of people who are interested in the same thing, such as chess or riding.

clumsy Someone who is clumsy moves or handles things awkwardly, so that things get broken or knocked over.

coach
1 A coach is a large vehicle which carries people on journeys by road.
2 A coach drawn by horses is a closed-in vehicle that used to carry passengers. Coaches are still used at special times.
3 If someone coaches you they train you for a sport, or give you extra lessons.

coal is a kind of hard black rock which is dug out of the ground and burned to give heat.

coast The coast is the place where land meets sea.

coat
1 A coat is a piece of clothing with long sleeves, that you wear over your other clothes when you go out.
2 An animal's coat is its fur or hair.
3 A thin layer of paint is called a coat: *Put another coat of paint on the door.*

cobweb A cobweb is a net made by a spider to trap insects.

cock A cock is any male bird.

cocoa
1 Cocoa is a brown powder made from the seeds of the cacao tree.
2 Cocoa is also a hot drink made from cocoa powder and milk or water.

coconut A coconut is a fruit which has a hard hairy shell. Inside there is a milky juice and white flesh that you can eat. It grows in tropical countries on a coconut palm tree.

cod A cod is a large sea fish which is caught for food.

coffee
1 Coffee is a coarse powder made by grinding roasted coffee beans.
2 Coffee is also a hot drink made by pouring water on to ground coffee.

coin A coin is a small piece of metal used as money.

cold (colder, coldest)
1 A cold is a common illness. If you have a cold you sneeze and your nose feels blocked.
2 If the weather is cold, the temperature outside is low.
3 Cold food is food that is meant to be eaten cold, such as a salad.

collapse If something collapses it suddenly falls down.

collar
1 The collar of a shirt or jacket is the part that fits around your neck.
2 A collar for a dog or cat is a band or chain that is put round its neck.

collect If you collect a number of things, you bring them together: *She collected sticks for firewood.*

college A college is a place where people go to study something, usually after they have left school.

colour The colour of something is the way it looks in daylight.

comb
1 A comb is a flat piece of plastic or metal with narrow teeth all along one edge. You tidy your hair with it.
2 A comb is also a fleshy crest on the head of some birds such as chickens.

combine harvester This is a large farm machine. As it is driven through a cornfield it cuts, sorts and cleans the grain.

comfortable Furniture that is comfortable is nice to use. If clothes such as shoes or trousers are comfortable, they fit well.

comic A comic is a magazine that tells stories in pictures.

common (commoner, commonest) If something is common, you often see it or it often happens.

common sense If you only need common sense to do something, you do not need any special knowledge.

company
1 A company is a group of people who work together making or selling things.
2 If you keep someone company you stay with them because they do not want to be on their own.

compare When you compare two or more things you look at them to see in what ways they are the same or different.

compass
1 A compass is an instrument with a needle that always points to north.
2 A compass is also an instrument for drawing circles.

complete
1 If you complete a job, you finish it.
2 If you talk about a complete thing, you mean all of it: *She grew out of her school clothes, and had to have a complete new outfit.*

computer A computer is a machine that stores information and works things out according to instructions in a programme.

concentrate If you concentrate on something you give all your attention to it.

concert A concert is a performance by musicians, usually in a big hall.

concrete is a building material made of cement, sand, small stones and water, which goes very hard when it is set.

cone A cone is a solid shape that is rounded at the bottom and pointed at the top.

confuse If you confuse two things you mix them up by mistake: *I always confuse leopards and cheetahs because they both have spots.*

connect If you connect two things, you join them together.

consonant A consonant is any letter of the alphabet except a, e, i, o, u.

constable A constable is a policeman.

construct If you construct something, you build it or make it.

container A container is something you put things in.

control is the ability to make something behave exactly as you want it to.

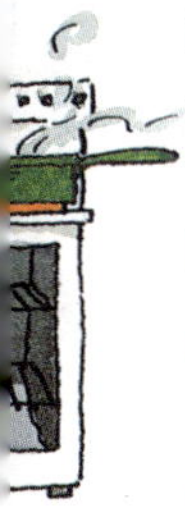

cooker A cooker is used to heat food. The inside is called the oven, and is used for roasting and baking. The top of the cooker is called the hob, and is used for boiling or frying.

cool (cooler, coolest)
1 If something is cool, its temperature is low, but it is not cold.
2 If you leave something hot to cool, you wait for it to get cooler.

copier A copier is a machine that makes copies of writing or pictures on paper.

copper is a reddish brown metal.

copy A copy is something that is made to look like something else.

cork A cork is a piece of cork or plastic used to block the open end of a bottle.

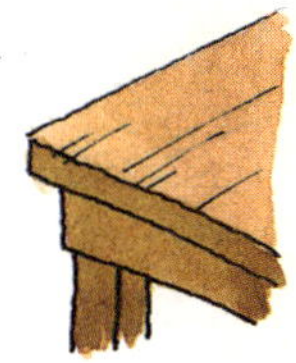

corn In Britain, corn is a crop such as wheat or barley. Corn is grown so that the seeds can be used as food. The seeds are called grain.

corner
1 The corner of something is the place where two edges or sides join.
2 The corner of a street is the place where two roads meet.
3 If you corner a person or animal, you get them into a place they cannot get out of easily.

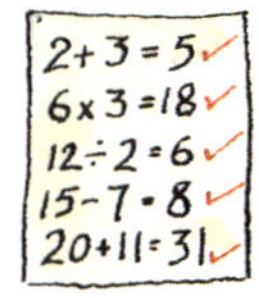

correct
1 Something that is correct does not have any mistakes in it.
2 If what you say is correct, it is true.

corridor A corridor is a long passage in a building or train.

cost
1 The cost of something is the amount of money needed to pay for it.
2 If something costs an amount of money, you can buy it for that amount.

costume A costume is special set of clothes worn by an actor or someone at a fancy dress party.

cot A cot is a bed with high sides for a baby or a young child.

cottage A cottage is a small house, usually in the country.

cotton
1 Cotton is a tall plant that is grown in hot countries. It has soft fine hairs (called fibres) round its seeds.
2 Cotton is a cloth woven from the soft fibres of the cotton plant.
3 Cotton is also a thread for sewing made from cotton fibres.

cough A cough is a noise made by someone forcing air out of their throat.

count
1 When you count, you say all the numbers one after the other
2 A count is a European nobleman.
3 If you count a number of people or things, you add them up to see how many there are.

counter
1 A counter is a long narrow table in a shop, where things are sold.
2 A counter is also a small round flat piece of something like plastic that is used in board games.

country
1 A country is a land that has its own government and language.
2 The country is land away from towns, where there are fields, trees and farms.

couple
1 Two people are sometimes called a couple, especially if they are married.
2 A couple of things means a few. You say this when the exact number does not really matter.

cover
1 The covers on a bed are the blankets or duvet that you have over you to keep you warm.
2 The cover of a book or magazine is the outside of it.

cow A cow is a large farm animal that gives milk.

crab A crab is a sea creature. It has a flat, roundish body covered by a shell, and five pairs of legs with large claws on the front pair.

crack
1 A crack is a very narrow gap between two things.
2 A crack is also a line on something breakable that shows it is slightly damaged.

cracker
1 A cracker is a thin crisp biscuit, often slightly salty.
2 A cracker is also a small firework that makes a noise when you light it.

cradle A cradle is a small bed for a baby.

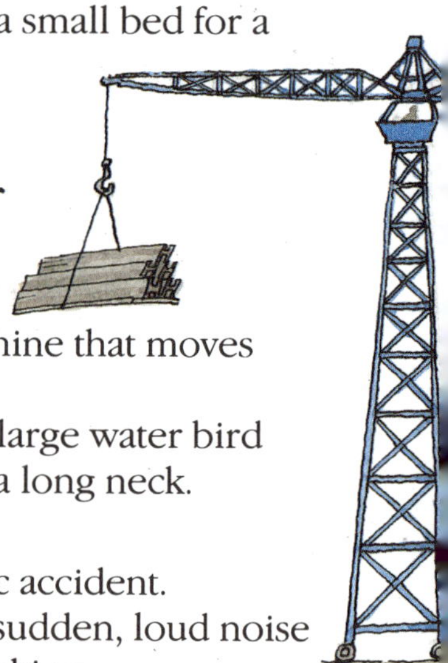

crane
1 A crane is a machine that moves heavy things.
2 A crane is also a large water bird with long legs and a long neck.

crash
1 A crash is a traffic accident.
2 A crash is also a sudden, loud noise like something breaking.

crawl When you crawl, you move forward on your hands and knees.

crayon A crayon is a coloured pencil.

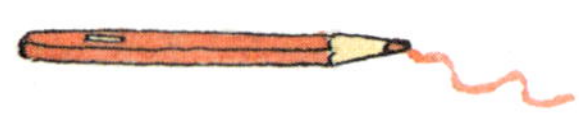

cream Cream is the pale yellow liquid that you find on top of milk. It is a little thicker than milk. You can buy cream on its own, to use in cooking or to pour over fruit or puddings.

creek
1 A creek is a strip of water where the sea comes a long way into the land.
2 In America, Canada, Australia, and New Zealand, a creek is a small stream.

creep If you creep somewhere, you move quietly and slowly: *You will have to creep about because Daddy's asleep.*

crew A crew is made up of people who work on a ship, aircraft or spaceship.

cricket
1 Cricket is an outdoor game between two teams of eleven players.
2 A cricket is a small jumping insect that makes a chirping sound by rubbing its wings together.

crisp (crisper, crispest)
1 A crisp is a thinly sliced piece of potato which is fried until it is crunchy.
2 Fruit and vegetables that are crisp are fresh and firm, so that when you bite them they are crunchy.

crocodile A crocodile is a large reptile, about 5 metres long.

crocus A crocus is a small plant that flowers in the spring. It can be white, yellow or purple.

crooked Something that is crooked is bent and twisted.

crop A crop is food such as corn or potatoes that is grown in fields.

cross
1 A cross is a sign like the letter X. People use it to show that something like a sum is wrong, or to mark a box on a form.
2 If you cross something like a road, you go from one side to the other.
3 If you cross your arms or legs, you put one on top of the other.
4 Someone who is cross usually frowns and speaks sharply.

crow A crow is a large black bird with a loud, harsh call.

crowd A crowd is a large number of people together in one place.

crown A crown is a precious ornament that kings and queens sometimes wear on their head.

cruel (crueller, cruellest) Someone who is cruel hurts people or animals without caring.

crumb A crumb is a very small piece of dry food such as bread or biscuit.

crush If you crush something you press it very hard. It may break or change its shape.

crust The crust is a hard layer on the outside of something, such as bread.

cry A cry is a sudden sound that you make when you are surprised or hurt.

crystal A crystal is a mineral that has formed into a regular shape: *They watched snow crystals falling on the window.*

cub A cub is a young wild animal, such as a lion, fox or bear.

cube A cube is a solid with six square sides.

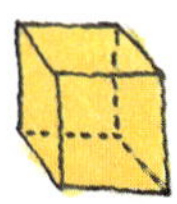

cuckoo A cuckoo is a grey bird, about 33 cm long.

cucumber A cucumber is a long thin vegetable with a dark green skin and pale green flesh. It is used for salads and sandwiches.

cup
1 A cup is a small container, usually with a handle. People drink liquids such as tea or coffee from a cup.
2 A cup is also a prize for the winner of a game or a competition.

cupboard A cupboard is a piece of furniture used for storing things like food or cups and saucers.

cure A cure is something that makes people better when they have been ill or injured.

curious
1 Someone who is curious is interested in things and wants to find out about them.
2 Something that is curious is unusual and interesting.

curl
1 Curls are pieces of hair shaped in curves and circles.
2 When something like a leaf curls, its edges roll in towards the middle.
3 If an animal curls up, it makes itself into a rounded shape.

currant
1 A currant is a small soft fruit such as a redcurrant or a blackcurrant.
2 Currants are small dried grapes, often used in fruit cakes.

current
1 A current is a steady movement of water or air.
2 A current is also the movement of electricity through a wire.

curtain A curtain is a piece of material that hangs from the top of a window. You pull it across the window to cover it.

curve
1 A curve is a smooth, gradually bending line.
2 A curved object has the shape of a curve: *The curved tusks of an elephant.*

cushion A cushion is a bag filled with soft material. You use cushions to sit on or lean back on.

cut
1 If you cut yourself, you hurt yourself by accident on something sharp. The skin is broken and you bleed.
2 If somebody cuts something they push a knife through it and take a piece out: *She cut the cake and gave him a piece.*

3 If someone cuts something like hair or a hedge, they take pieces off to make it tidy.

cycle A cycle is a bicycle.

daffodil A daffodil is a yellow, trumpet-shaped flower that blooms in the spring.

daily Something that happens daily happens every day.

dairy A dairy is a shop or company that sells milk and food made from milk, such as butter and cheese.

daisy A daisy is a small, common wild flower with white or pink petals and a yellow centre.

dam A dam is a wall built across a river or stream. The dam stops the water flowing, and makes a lake.

damage If something causes damage to something else, it spoils or breaks it so that it does not work properly or look as good as it did before: *The storm caused a lot of damage to houses in the area.*

damp (damper, dampest) Something that is damp is slightly wet.

dance A dance is made up of movements of the whole body, usually in time to music.

danger A danger is something that could harm you.

dangerous If something is dangerous it is likely to harm you: *Frozen ponds are very dangerous because the ice might crack.*

dark
1 When it is dark there is not enough light to see properly.
2 If you say someone has dark hair, you mean their hair is brown or black.

dart
1 A dart is like a small arrow. It has a sharp point and is used in a game called darts.
2 If a person or an animal darts somewhere they move suddenly and quickly.

date If someone asks you the date you tell them the day and the month: *It is 7th August.*

dawn is the time of day when it first begins to get light.

day
1 A day is the time between one midnight and the next. There are 24 hours in one day.
2 If you say you will do something during the day, you will do it between getting up and going to bed.

daytime is the part of the day when it is light.

dazzle If a light dazzles you, you cannot see properly for a short time.

deaf Someone who is deaf cannot hear very well, or cannot hear at all.

dear (dearer, dearest)
1 When you are writing a letter, you begin with 'Dear', and then put the name of the person you are writing to.
2 If something is dear it costs a lot of money.

death is the end of the life of a person or animal.

deceive If someone deceives you, they make you believe something that is not true.

December is the twelfth month of the year. It has thirty-one days.

decide If you decide to do something, you make up your mind to do it.

deck A deck is one of the floors on a ship or a bus.

decorate
1 If you decorate something you make it more attractive by adding some kind of ornament: *I'm going to decorate the tree with fairy lights.*
2 If someone decorates a room they paper it or paint it.

deed A deed is something that is done, usually very good or very bad.

deep (deeper, deepest) If something is deep, it goes a long way down: *The river is very deep here.*

deer A deer is a large, wild animal that eats grass and leaves.

defeat If you defeat someone, you win in something such as a game or battle.

defend If you defend somebody or something, you do something to keep them safe.

delicious Food that is delicious tastes or smells very nice.

deliver If you deliver something, you hand it to somebody.

dent If somebody dents something smooth, they make a dip in it by hitting it: *He drove into the garage too fast and dented his bumper.*

deposit If you put a deposit on something you want to buy, you pay part of the money. The shop then keeps it for you until you pay the rest.

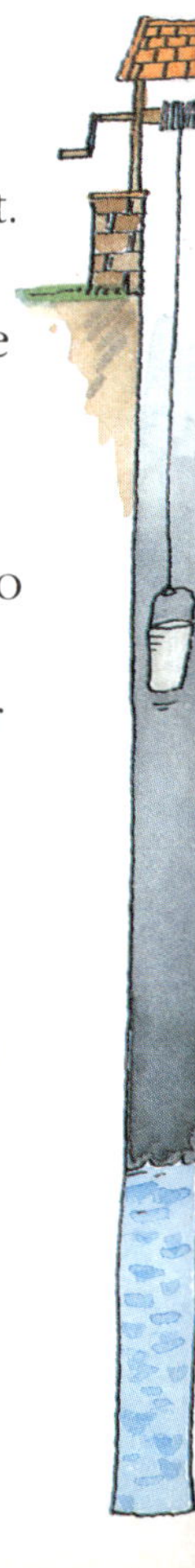

depth
1 The depth of something like a lake or a hole is the distance from top to bottom.
2 The depth of something like a cupboard is the distance from front to back.

describe If you describe a person or thing, you say what they are like.

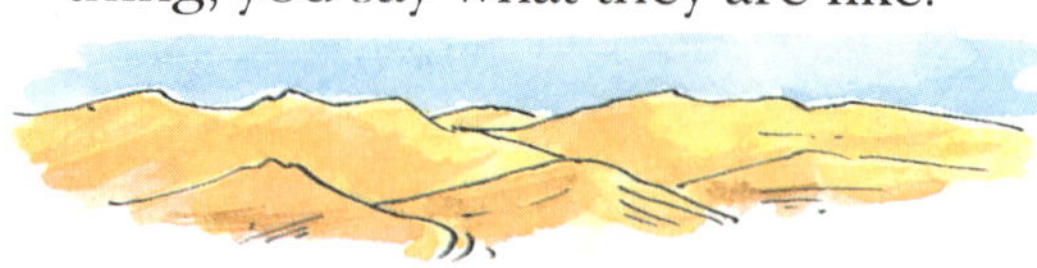

desert A desert is a large area of land where there is very little water or rain, so hardly any plants can grow.

deserve If you deserve something, you earn it by what you have done.

desk A desk is a special table people use for writing or reading. Desks often have drawers in them.

destroy If somebody destroys something, they damage it so much that it cannot be repaired.

dew is small drops of water that cover the ground early in the morning.

diagonal A diagonal is a sloping line.

dial A dial is a numbered disc on an instrument like a clock or a speedometer.

diamond
1 A diamond is a very hard precious stone. When it has been cut it sparkles.
2 A diamond is also a shape with four straight sides, like a square but slightly flattened.

diary A diary is a book which has a space for each day. You use a diary to make a note of special dates like your next visit to the dentist, or things you have been doing during the day.

dice A dice is a small cube made of something like wood or plastic. It has spots on each of its six sides.

dictionary A dictionary is a book in which words are listed in an alphabetical order. It tells you what the words mean, and helps you to check the spelling.

diesel A diesel is a vehicle that has a diesel engine. A diesel engine burns a special oil instead of petrol.

different Something that is different from something else is not like it in one or more ways.

difficult
1 Something that is difficult is not easy to do.
2 If something is difficult to understand, you cannot understand it without thinking very hard about it.

dig When people dig they push something like a spade into the ground, to make a hole or to move the earth to somewhere else. When animals dig, they use their claws to make a hole.

dim If the light is dim, it is rather dark and it is hard to see things.

dining room The dining room is the place in a house or hotel where people have their meals.

dinner is the main meal of the day.

dinosaur A dinosaur was a large reptile which lived and became extinct in prehistoric times.

direct Direct means in a straight line without stopping, as on a journey: *Is this the direct train to London?*

dirty Something that is dirty is marked or covered with mud or stains and needs to be cleaned.

disagree If you disagree with someone, you think that what they are saying is wrong.

disappear If someone disappears, they go out of sight.

disappoint When things or people disappoint you, you are unhappy because what you were hoping for did not happen.

disc A disc is something flat and round.

discover When you discover something you did not know before, you find out about it.

discuss When you discuss something you talk about it to someone else.

disease A disease is an illness in people, animals or plants.

dish A dish is a shallow container for cooking or serving meals.

dishonest If someone is dishonest, they are not to be trusted.

dishwasher A dishwasher is a machine that washes and dries things like plates and saucepans.

dislike If you dislike someone or something, you think they are unpleasant and you do not like them.

disobey If someone disobeys, they do not do what they have been told to do.

distance The distance between two points is the amount of space between them.

disturb If you disturb someone you interrupt their peace and quiet.

ditch A ditch is a long narrow channel dug at the side of a road or field, to drain water.

dive When swimmers dive, they jump headfirst into water, with their hands above their head.

dodge If you dodge, you move suddenly out of the way.

dog A dog is an animal that is often kept as a pet, or used to hunt or guard things.

doll A doll is a child's toy that looks like a small person or baby.

dollar A dollar is a unit of money in some countries such as the USA, Canada and Australia.

dolphin A dolphin is a kind of whale measuring about 2-3 metres. Dolphins are friendly, intelligent animals that live in groups in the Mediterranean and the Atlantic.

donkey A donkey is a kind of ass, and belongs to the horse family. It is smaller than a horse, with longer ears. The noise it makes is called a bray.

door A door is usually made of something like wood, glass or metal. It swings or slides to open and close a cupboard, room or building.

double
1 If something is double the size or amount of something else, it is twice as big.
2 You say double when there are two of the same kind: *That egg had a double yolk.*

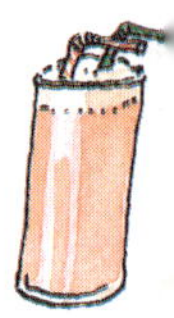

doubt (say dowt) If you have a doubt about something, you are not sure about it: *There is some doubt about what we shall do if it rains.*

dough is a floury mixture that can be cooked to make things like pastry or bread. It has a soft rubbery feel.

doughnut A doughnut is a small cake of sweet dough that has been cooked in hot fat. Doughnuts sometimes have jam in, and sometimes have a hole in the middle.

down is small soft feathers that grow on young birds. It is used to fill pillows or duvets.

drag
1 If you drag something along, you pull it along the ground because it is too heavy to carry.
2 If you drag yourself away from something, you force yourself to leave although you do not want to.

dragon In stories a dragon is an animal like a big lizard. It has wings and claws and breathes out fire.

drain
1 A drain is a pipe that carries water away.
2 If a liquid drains away it flows slowly to somewhere else.

draught A draught is a stream of air coming into a room or vehicle.

draughts is a game for two people, played with 24 round pieces on a special board.

draw When you draw you use something like a pencil or crayon to make a picture or a pattern.

drawbridge A drawbridge is a bridge that can be pulled up to stop people getting into a castle.

drawer A drawer is a box that slides in and out of a piece of furniture.

drawing pin A drawing pin is a short nail with a flat top. You pin papers to a board by pressing it with your thumb.

dreadful Something that is dreadful is very bad or unpleasant.

dream A dream is the pictures and sounds that happen in your mind when you are asleep.

dress
1 A dress is a piece of clothing worn by women and girls. It covers their body, and the hem reaches to somewhere on their legs.
2 When you dress, or get dressed, you put on your clothes.

drill A drill is a tool or machine for making holes.

drink
1 A drink is a liquid which is all right to swallow.
2 When you drink you take liquid into your mouth and swallow it.

drip When something drips, drops of liquid fall from it one after the other: *The tap is dripping. Will you please turn it off properly?*

drive If someone drives a vehicle they make it work and steer it where they want it to go.

drop
1 A drop is a small amount of liquid shaped like a little ball.
2 If you drop something, you let it fall, usually by accident.
3 If the temperature drops you feel colder.

drown If someone drowns they die because they have gone under water and cannot breathe.

drum
1 A drum is a musical instrument shaped like a cylinder. It has skin stretched tightly over the end, and you beat it with sticks or your hand.
2 A drum is also a large cylinder for holding oil.

dry (drier, driest) Something that is dry has no moisture in it.

duck A duck is a common water bird with short legs and webbed feet.

duet A duet is a piece of music played or sung by two people.

dull Something that is dull is not very interesting.

during Something that happens during a period of time happens for the whole of that period: *I went to school during the summer holidays.*

dusk is the part of the day when it is just beginning to get dark.

dust
1 Dust is very small dry pieces of earth or sand that fly up from roads when traffic goes by.
2 Dust is also fine powdered dirt that you find inside the house on things like floors and furniture.

dustbin A dustbin is a metal or plastic container with a lid, that people keep outside their houses to put rubbish in.

duster A duster is a soft cloth for removing dust from things like furniture and ornaments.

duvet (say doovay) is a bed cover filled with feathers or other lightweight material.

dwarf
1 A dwarf is a person who is much smaller than other people.
2 In fairy stories, a dwarf is a small creature who often has magic powers.

eager If you are eager to do something, you want to do it very much.

eagle An eagle is a large strong bird with a sharp curved beak and talons. It kills small animals for food.

ear Your ears are the part of your body that you use for hearing.

earn If you earn something such as money, you get it by working for it.

earring An earring is a piece of jewellery that is fixed to the ear for decoration. Earrings are usually sold in pairs.

earth
1 The earth is the planet we live on.
2 Earth is the soil that plants grow in.
3 An earth is a hole in the ground where an animal such as a fox lives.

earthquake An earthquake is a shaking of the ground caused by movement of the earth's crust.

easel An easel is a stand to hold a blackboard or a picture that an artist is painting.

east is one of the four main points of the compass: *She looked towards the east to watch the sun rise.*

easy Something that is easy can be done without difficulty.

eat
1 When you eat, you put food in your mouth, chew it and swallow it.
2 To eat also means to have a meal.

echo An echo is a sound that bounces back from something like the walls of a cave or building.

eclipse An eclipse of the sun happens when the moon comes between the earth and the sun, so that for a short time you cannot see all or part of the sun.

edge
1 An edge is the end of a flat object such as a table or a book.
2 The edge of a large area is the place where it stops and another area begins: *They played at the water's edge.*

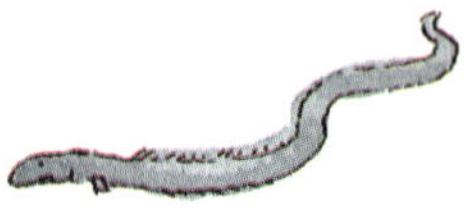

eel An eel is a long thin fish that looks like a snake. Young eels are called elvers.

egg An egg is an oval object laid by female birds and some other animals and insects.

elastic is a rubber material that stretches when you pull it and springs back to its normal size when you let it go.

elbow Your elbow is the joint in the middle of your arm where it bends.

electricity is a form of energy that is used for heating and lighting. It also powers equipment such as fridges and irons.

elephant An elephant is a very large animal with a long nose called a trunk, which it uses to pick up things. An adult elephant has tusks of ivory at each side of its mouth. Elephants live in groups called herds in India and Africa. Baby elephants are called calves.

elevator
1 An elevator is a lift that carries people up and down inside buildings.
2 An elevator is also a machine used for lifting heavy objects in a place like a warehouse.

elf In fairy stories, an elf is a tiny boy who can do magic things.

emerald
1 An emerald is a bright green precious stone.
2 Emerald also means bright green in colour.

emergency An emergency is something difficult and sometimes dangerous that happens unexpectedly.

empty
1 Something such as a box, vehicle or room that is empty has no people or things in it.
2 If you empty a container, you pour or take everything out of it.

enemy Your enemy is someone who fights against you.

energy
1 Energy is the strength to do things.
2 Energy is also the power from things like electricity that makes machines work.

engine
1 An engine is a machine that uses heat or other kinds of energy to make a vehicle move.
2 An engine is also a large vehicle that pulls a railway train.

enjoy If you enjoy doing something, you like doing it very much.

enormous Something that is enormous is very, very large.

enough If you have enough of something you have as much as you need: *If I have two more sheets of paper that will be enough.*

entertain If you entertain somebody, you do something that they enjoy and find amusing.

entertainment is something like a show or a film that people watch for pleasure.

entrance An entrance is the way into a place.

envelope An envelope is a folded paper cover for something like a letter or a card.

equal If things are equal, they are the same as each other in size, number or amount: *100 centimetres equal 1 metre.*

equator The equator is an imaginary line drawn around the centre of the earth, at an equal distance from the North Pole and the South Pole.

equipment is the things that are used for a particular purpose: *They needed new kitchen equipment, so they looked at cookers and fridges.*

error If you have made an error, something you have done is not quite right: *She wrote a nice letter, but there were two spelling errors.*

escape If a person or an animal escapes, they get away from whatever is holding them: *The hamster escaped from its cage.*

evening The evening is the part of the day between the end of the afternoon and the time when you go to bed.

ever means at any time in the past or future: *Have you ever seen such a big dog?*

evergreen An evergreen is a tree or other plant that has leaves all the year round.

evil If someone is evil they are very wicked and like doing things that hurt other people.

exactly
1 You can say exactly when you mean no more and no less: *My father is exactly two metres tall.*
2 Exactly also means just right: *He found a piece that fitted exactly.*

examination An examination is a test that people take to show how much they have learned.

examine
1 If you examine something, you look at it carefully or closely.
2 If a doctor examines you, he or she looks at you carefully to see whether there is anything wrong with your health.
3 To examine someone means to find out how much they know by giving them a test.

example
1 An example is one person or thing that shows what the rest of a set is like: *This is an example of my work.*
2 If you set an example, you behave so that others will copy you.

excellent Something that is excellent is very, very good.

excite If something excites you, you feel happy and unable to rest.

excitement is a feeling of being very happy and nervous.

excuse (as in juice) An excuse is a reason you give for doing something, or not doing it.

exercise
1 Exercises are regular movements you make to keep fit.
2 An exercise is a short piece of work that you do in school to help you learn something such as arithmetic.

exit
1 An exit is the way out of a large public building such as a theatre.
2 A motorway exit is a point where traffic can leave the motorway.

expect If you expect something, you think it will happen.

explain When you explain, you say something that will help people to understand.

explode If something such as a firework explodes it bursts with a loud bang.

express
1 An express is a fast train or coach which does not stop at many places.
2 If you express an idea or feeling, you put it into words, or show it by the way you act: *He could only express the way he felt by bursting into tears.*

expression Your expression is a look on your face that lets people know what you are thinking or feeling.

extinct If an animal or plant family is extinct, it no longer has any living members: *The dodo has been extinct for more than 300 years.*

eye The eyes are the parts of a person's or animal's body that are used for seeing.

eyebrow Your eyebrows are the lines of hair which grow above each eye.

eyelash Your eyelashes are the hairs which grow on the edge of your eyelids.

eyelid Your eyelids are the pieces of skin which cover your eyes when you close them.

eyesight is the ability to see.

fabric is a material like cloth that is made in some way such as weaving or knitting.

face
1 Your face is the front part of your head from your chin to the top of your forehead.
2 The face of a clock or watch is the part with the numbers on it that shows the time.

fact A fact is something that is true.

factory A factory is a large building where a lot of things are made, usually with the help of machines.

fade
1 When a colour fades, it gets paler.
2 When the light fades, it gets darker, usually because the sun is going down.

fail
1 If someone fails when they try to do something, they cannot do it.
2 If something fails it stops working, or does not do what it is supposed to do: *The brakes failed, and the car hit a wall.*

failure If something is a failure, it is disappointing: *The picnic was a failure – it rained all day.*

faint
1 Something like a sound or mark that is faint is not easy to hear or see.
2 If someone faints they become unconscious for a short time.

fair
1 A fair is an outside entertainment, where exciting things like roundabouts are set up for a few days so that people can have fun.
2 Something that is fair seems reasonable to most people.

faithful Someone who is faithful to a person or a group of people can be trusted to do their best for them.

fall
1 If someone or something falls, they suddenly drop towards the ground.
2 When night falls, it becomes dark.
3 In America, fall is the autumn, when leaves start to fall.

false
1 If something you say is false, it is not true.
2 If something is false, it is not the real thing: *Her grandfather lost a front tooth and had to have a false one.*

family
1 A family is a group of people made up of parents and their children.
1 A family is also a group of animals or plants of the same kind: *Weasels, stoats and otters all belong to the weasel family.*

famine When there is a famine in a country, there is little or no food, usually because the crops have failed.

famous Someone who is famous is very well known.

fan A fan is a flat object, usually made of folded paper. You wave a fan to move the air and make yourself feel cooler.

fang Fangs are long sharp teeth.

far (farther, farthest) Far means a long way away.

fare A fare is the money that you pay for a journey in something like a plane or a train.

farm A farm is a large area of land that is used for growing crops or keeping animals. A farm also has buildings on it, such as a house where the farmer lives, and barns for storing things in.

fast (faster, fastest)
1 Someone or something that is fast can move very quickly.
2 If a watch or clock is fast, it is moving too quickly and shows a time that is later than the real time.
3 If someone fasts, they eat no food for a period of time.
4 Something that is held fast is firmly fixed.

fasten When you fasten something you close it or do it up with something like a button, strap or catch: *Remember to fasten your safety belt.*

fat (fatter, fattest)
1 Fat is the extra flesh that people and animals have under their skin. It is used to store energy and to help keep them warm.
2 Fat is also a solid or liquid that comes from animals or vegetables, which is used in cooking.
3 A person or animal that is fat has too much flesh on their body.

fault
1 A fault is something wrong with the way something was made: *All those cars had the same fault.*
2 If people say something is your fault, they are blaming you for something bad that happened.
3 If you find fault with somebody, you look for mistakes and talk about them unkindly.

favour A favour is something kind you do for someone because they have asked you to.

favourite Your favourite is the one you like best of a number of people or things: *This teddy is my favourite toy.*

fear is the nasty feeling you have when you think you are in danger.

feast A feast is a large and special meal to which lots of people are invited.

feather A feather is one of the very light pieces that make up a bird's coat.

February is the second month of the year. It has 28 days except in a leap year, when it has 29.

feeble Someone who is feeble does not have much strength or energy.

feed
1 If you feed a person or animal, you give them food.
2 If you feed a plant you give it something special to make it grow well.

feel
1 If you feel something like happy, excited or sad, that is the way you are at that time.
2 If you feel an object you touch it to find out something about it, such as whether it is rough or smooth.

felt is a material made from threads of something like wool packed tightly together to make a thick cloth.

female A female is a person or animal that can become a mother.

fence A fence is something that divides two areas of land. It is usually made of wood or wire stretched between wooden posts.

ferry A ferry is a boat that takes passengers and sometimes vehicles across a short stretch of water.

festival A festival is a date or time of the year when people have a holiday because of something special.

fetch If you fetch something, you go and get it and bring it back.

fever If you have a fever when you are ill, you have a high temperature.

few A few things or people means a small number of them: *I looked carefully, and found a few fossils.*

fibre A fibre is a thin thread of something such as wool, cotton or nylon.

field A field is land where crops are grown, or an area of rough grass where horses, sheep or cattle are kept.

fierce A person who is fierce looks or sounds angry.

fight If you fight you try to hurt someone in some way such as hitting them with your fists.

figure
1 A figure is any of the numbers from 0 to 9: *There are two figures in the number of my house. It is number 23.*
2 You say you can see a figure when you can see someone, but not very clearly: *It was just getting dark when I saw a small figure coming towards me.*

fill If you fill something, you put so much into it there is no room for any more.

film
1 A film is moving pictures shown on a screen.
2 Film is a long narrow piece of plastic that is used in a camera to take photographs.

filthy (filthier, filthiest) If something is filthy it is very, very dirty.

fin A fish's fins are like small wings that stick out of its body. They help the fish to swim and to keep its balance.

find When you find somebody or something you see what you have been looking for.

fine (finer, finest)
1 A fine is money that is paid as a punishment.
2 Something that is fine is very good indeed.
3 If you say you are fine, you mean you are well and happy.

finger Your fingers are the four long, jointed parts at the end of your hand. Sometimes when people say fingers they mean thumbs as well.

finish
1 The finish of something like a race is the end of it.
2 When you finish something like a meal you reach the end of it.

fir A fir is a tall, pointed, evergreen tree with leaves like needles. Firs have cones which carry their seeds.

fire
1 A fire is a burning pile of coal or wood that people make to keep warm.
2 A fire is also something powered by gas or electricity that gives out heat.
3 Fire is the hot bright flames made by something that is burning.
4 If someone fires a gun, a bullet is sent from the gun they are using.

fireplace A fireplace is a space at the bottom of a wall in a room. It has a chimney leading out of it so that the smoke can escape when a fire is lit.

firework A firework is a small object that burns with coloured flames or sparks when you light it. Some fireworks make a loud noise, and some shoot up into the air. Sometimes people let off a lot of fireworks when it is a special day.

firm (firmer, firmest)
1 A firm is a company that makes or sells something.
2 Something that is firm does not change much in shape when you press it, but is not completely hard.

first aid is a simple treatment given as soon as possible to a person who is injured or who suddenly becomes ill.

fish A fish is a creature that lives in water. It has fins and a tail. There are many different kinds of fish.

fisherman A fisherman is a person who catches fish. Some people catch fish for food, and some do it for sport.

fishing is the sport, hobby or job of catching fish.

fist You make a fist by tucking your fingers into the palm of your hand. You usually do this if you are cross, or are holding something tightly: *She held the money tightly in her fist.*

fit (fitter, fittest)
1 If you have a fit of something like coughing, you suddenly start doing it and find it hard to stop.
2 If something such as clothing fits you, it is the right size for you.
3 Someone who is fit is healthy.

fix
1 If you fix something somewhere, you put it there firmly so that it cannot be moved: *He fixed a lamp to the wall outside.*
2 If you fix something that has broken, you make it work again.

flag A flag is a piece of cloth that can be fixed to a pole as a sign, signal or symbol of something. Each country in the world has a different flag, made with special colours or patterns.

flame A flame is burning gas that comes from anything that is burning or on fire. Flames are very hot and bright.

flannel
1 Flannel is a warm, lightweight cloth woven from something like wool. Suits are sometimes made from flannel.
2 A flannel is a small piece of towelling that people use to wash themselves.

flap
1 A flap is something flat that is fixed along one edge so that the rest of it can move freely: *The cat can get out through a flap in the door.*
2 If something like paper or cloth flaps it moves quickly up and down, or from side to side, often making a snapping sound.
3 When a bird flaps its wings, it moves them up and down quickly.

flash
1 A flash is a very bright light which comes suddenly and only lasts a moment, like lightning in a storm.
2 If something flashes past, it moves so fast that you cannot see it properly.

flask
1 A flask is a flat container made of metal or glass for carrying something to drink with you.
2 A Thermos flask is specially made to keep drinks hot or cold.

flat (flatter, flattest)
1 Something that is flat is level. It does not slope or curve, or have any bumps or wrinkles in it.
2 A flat is a set of rooms for living in. It is usually on one floor, and is part of a larger building. A flat usually has a kitchen and bathroom.

flavour
1 The flavour of food or drink is what it tastes like.
2 If you flavour food or drink you add something to it to give it a special taste.

flesh
1 Flesh is the soft part of a person's or animal's body that covers the bones and is underneath the skin.
2 The flesh of a fruit or vegetable is the soft part of it.

flight
1 A flight is a journey made in an aircraft.
2 The flight of a bird is the act of flying.
3 If a bird has flight it is able to fly.
4 A flight of stairs or steps is a set that leads from one level to another without changing direction.

flippers
1 The flippers of an animal such as a seal or a penguin are the flat limbs that it uses for swimming.
2 Flippers are flat pieces of rubber that you can wear on your feet to help you swim more quickly.

float
1 If something floats in a liquid it rests on it, moving slowly.
2 If something floats through the air, it moves gently above the ground.

flock A flock of birds or sheep is a group of them.

flood A flood is a large amount of water which covers an area that is usually dry.

floor
1 The floor of a room is the flat part that you walk on.
2 A floor of a building is all the rooms at that level: *My flat is on the third floor.*

flour is a white or brown powder made by grinding grain such as wheat. Flour is used to make things like bread and cakes.

flow If a liquid flows in a certain direction it moves in a steady stream.

flower A flower is the part of a plant which is often brightly coloured and only lasts for a short time.

flu is an illness which is like a very bad cold. You get a high temperature and ache all over. Flu is short for influenza.

fly
1 A fly is a small insect with two wings.
2 When a bird, insect or aircraft flies it moves through the air.
3 If you fly somewhere, you travel there in an aircraft.

fog When there is a fog there are tiny drops of water in the air which make a thick cloud so that it is difficult to see things.

fold
1 Folds in material are the curves in it when it does not hang flat: *The curtains hung in soft folds.*
2 When you fold something such as paper or cloth, you bend one part of it so that it covers another part, often pressing the edge so that it stays in place.

follow
1 If you follow someone who is moving you move along behind them.
2 If one thing follows another, it happens after it.
3 If you follow something like a path you go along it.

fond If you are fond of someone you like them very much.

food is what people and animals eat to stay alive, and what plants need to grow.

foot Your foot is the part of your body that touches the ground when you stand or walk.

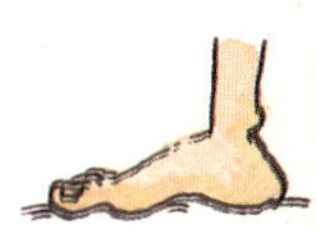

football
1 Football is a game played on a field between two teams who use a ball to try and win points against each other by scoring goals.
2 A football is a large ball filled with air that is used in games of football.

footstep A footstep is the sound or mark made by someone walking each time their foot touches the ground.

force The force of something is the powerful effect it has: *The force of the earthquake damaged hundreds of buildings.*

forecast
1 A weather forecast tells you what sort of weather to expect.
2 If someone forecasts something, they say what they think is going to happen in the future.

forehead Your forehead is the front part of your head between your hair and your eyebrows.

foreign Something that is foreign is to do with a country that is not your own.

forest A forest is a large area where trees grow close together.

forever Something that goes on forever never ends.

forget If you forget something, you cannot think of it, although you knew it before: *I'll write that down before I forget it.*

forgive If you forgive someone who has done something bad, you stop being cross with them.

fork
1 A fork is a tool that you use for eating food. It has three or four prongs on the end of a handle.
2 A fork is also a large tool that you use for digging in the garden.

form
1 A form is a piece of paper with questions on it and spaces where you should write the answers.
2 A form in a school is a class: *Her brother is in the sixth form.*
3 When something forms a particular shape it is arranged in such a way that this shape is made.

fort A fort is a strong building or a place with a wall or fence round it where soldiers can stay and be safe from the enemy.

fortnight A fortnight is a period of two weeks.

fortune
1 Fortune is good or bad luck.
2 Someone who tells your fortune says what they think will happen to you in the future.
3 If someone has a fortune, they have a lot of money.

fossil A fossil is the hardened remains of a prehistoric animal or plant that are found inside a rock.

fountain A fountain is a jet or spray of water forced up into the air by a pump.

fountain pen A fountain pen is a pen with a container inside which sends ink to the nib.

fowl A fowl is a bird, especially one that can be eaten, such as duck or chicken.

fox A fox is a wild animal which looks like a dog. It has reddish-brown fur and a thick tail.

fraction
1 A fraction is a tiny amount or part of something: *The door opened a fraction and the cat put its paw through.*
2 A fraction is also a measured part such as a half or a quarter of something.

fracture A fracture is a crack or break in something, especially a bone.

fragrant Something that is fragrant has a pleasant, sweet smell.

frame
1 A frame is an object made from long thin pieces of something such as wood. Frames are usually made with straight sides and a space in the middle.
2 The frames of a pair of glasses are the wire or plastic parts which hold the lenses in place.

free (freer, freest)
1 Someone who is free is not controlled by anybody.
2 If something is free, it does not cost anything.

freedom You have freedom if you are free.

freeze If a liquid freezes it becomes solid because the temperature is low.

freezer A freezer is a large container like a fridge where you can store food for a long time because the temperature inside is kept very low.

fresh
1 If food is fresh it has been gathered or made recently, and has not become stale or bad.
2 Fresh water is water that is not salty.
3 If you feel fresh, you feel rested and full of energy.
4 Fresh air is the air outside.

Friday is one of the seven days of the week.

fridge A fridge is a large metal container. It is kept cool so that the food in it stays fresh longer.

friend A friend is someone you know well and like very much.

friendly (friendlier, friendliest) Someone who is friendly behaves in a pleasant, kind way.

fright
1 Fright is a sudden feeling of fear.
2 If something gives you a fright, it makes you jump and feel very nervous.

frighten If something frightens you it makes you feel afraid.

frog A frog is a small creature with smooth skin, big eyes and long back legs which it uses for jumping. Frogs like to live near water, and their hind feet are webbed to help them swim.

frown When you frown your eyebrows are drawn together. People frown when they are annoyed or worried, or when they are thinking hard.

frozen
1 If a lake is frozen, its surface has turned to ice because the temperature is very low.
2 Frozen food has been preserved by bringing it to a very low temperature.

fruit A fruit is something you can eat that grows on a tree or bush. It contains seeds or a stone. Oranges, plums and grapes are fruit.

fry When you fry food you cook it in a pan that contains hot fat or oil.

fuel is something such as wood or coal that is burned to provide heat or power.

full If something is full, there is no room for anything more.

fun is something enjoyable that makes you feel happy: *Why don't we go on the bumper cars? That would be fun.*

funny (funnier, funniest)
1 Something that is funny is rather strange or surprising.
2 Funny people or things make you laugh.
3 If you say you feel funny you mean you don't feel very well.

fur is the thick hair that grows on the bodies of many mammals.

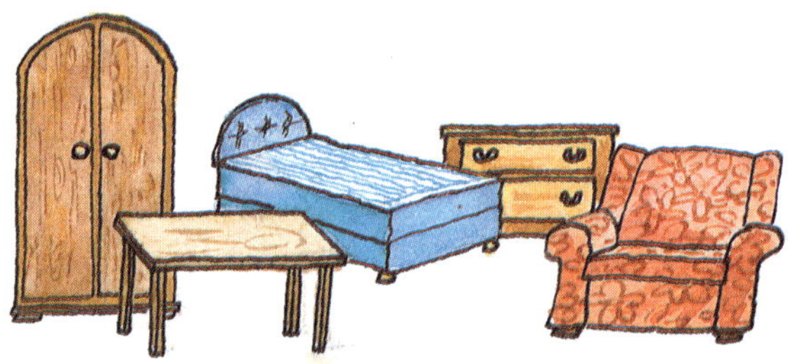

furniture means large moveable objects such as tables, beds and chairs that people have in their rooms.

fury
1 Fury is very strong anger.
2 If you are in a fury you are very angry.

future The future is the time that is to come.

gain
1 A gain is an increase in the amount of something: *He tried to lose weight, but the scales showed a gain of two kilos.*
2 If you gain from something you get something good out of it.

galaxy A galaxy is a group of stars and planets that spreads over many millions of miles.

galleon A galleon is a large sailing ship with heavy guns. Galleons were used mainly three or four hundred years ago.

gallery
1 A gallery is a place that shows paintings or sculpture.
2 In a hall or theatre, a gallery is a raised area at the back where people can sit and get a good view of what is happening.

galley A galley is a ship that was used for war hundreds of years ago. It had sails and many oars, and was rowed by slaves or prisoners.

gallop When a horse gallops it runs very fast so that all its legs are off the ground at the same time.

game
1 A game is a sport or something you play in which you follow fixed rules and try to win.
2 A game can also be something you play where you use toys or pretend to be someone else.

gang
1 A gang is a group of bad people who work together doing things that are against the law.
2 A gang can also mean a group of workers.

gap
1 A gap is an empty space between two things.
2 A gap can be a period of time when you are not doing what you usually do, or when you are not busy.

garage
1 A garage is a building in which someone can keep a car.
2 A garage is also a place where people buy petrol or get their cars repaired.

garden A garden is land next to someone's house where they can grow things such as trees, flowers or grass.

garment A garment is a piece of clothing, such as a shirt or coat.

gas is something like air that is neither liquid nor solid. It burns easily, and is used as a fuel for fires, cookers and central heating in people's homes.

gate A gate is a door that is used at the entrance to a field, garden or grounds of a building.

gather If people or animals gather, they come together in a group.

general
1 A general is an important officer in the armed forces.
2 You use the word general when you are talking about most people, or most of the people in a group.

generous Someone who is generous is kind and willing to help others by giving them what they can.

gentle Someone who is gentle is kind, calm and sensitive.

gently If you do something gently you are very careful.

geography is the study of the countries of the world and the people who live in them.

gerbil a gerbil is a small, furry animal with long back legs. Gerbils are often kept as pets.

germ A germ is a very small living thing that can make people ill. You cannot see germs without using a microscope.

ghost A ghost is a shadowy figure of someone no longer living that some people believe they see.

giant
1 In fairy stories, a giant is someone who is very, very large and strong.
2 Anything that is much larger than others of its kind can be called giant.

gift
1 A gift is something you give someone as a present.
2 If you say someone has a gift for doing something, you mean they have a natural ability for doing it.

gigantic Something that is gigantic is very, very large.

giraffe A giraffe is a large African animal with a very long neck, long legs, and dark patches on its yellowish skin. It is the tallest of all the mammals and can grow to nearly six metres. Giraffes live in herds in open country, eating leaves and young twigs.

girl A girl is a female child or young woman.

glacier A glacier is a huge mass of ice which moves very slowly, often down a mountain valley.

glad (gladder, gladdest)
1 If you are glad about something you are happy and pleased about it.
2 If you say you are glad to do something, you mean that you are willing and eager to do it.

glass
1 Glass is a hard and transparent material that is easily broken. It is used to make windows, and such things as bottles and bowls.
2 A glass is a drink container.

glasses are two lenses in a metal or plastic frame. People with bad eyesight wear them in front of their eyes to help them see properly.

glide When something glides it moves silently and smoothly: *She watched the swans glide past.*

glider A glider is an aircraft that does not have an engine, but flies by floating on air currents.

globe A globe is a round model of the Earth. It is usually fixed on a stand so that you can spin it round, and it has a map of the world drawn on it.

glove A glove is a piece of clothing which covers your hand, with separate places for each finger.

glue is a thick, sticky liquid used for joining things together, either when they are being made or if they are broken.

gnat (say nat) A gnat is a very small flying insect that bites people. Gnats usually live near water.

gnaw (say naw) If people or animals gnaw something, or gnaw at it, they bite on something hard for a long time: *The puppy spent the morning gnawing a bone.*

goal
1 A goal in games such as football or hockey is the space into which players try to get the ball so that they can score a point for their team.
2 If you score a goal you win a point by getting the ball into the goal.

goat A goat is an animal with short coarse hair, horns and a short tail.

goblin In fairy stories a goblin is a small ugly creature who likes to make trouble.

goggles are large glasses that fit closely around your eyes to protect them from things like dust, sparks or water.

golf is a game in which people use long sticks called clubs to hit a small ball into special holes. The game is played on a large area of grassy land which usually has eighteen holes.

good (better, best)
1 Someone who is good is kind and caring, and can be trusted.
2 A child or animal that is good is well-behaved and obedient.
3 Good music, art or literature is of high quality.
4 Something such as a film or a show that is good is pleasant and enjoyable.
5 Someone who is good at something is skilful and successful at it.

goodbye You say goodbye to someone when you or they are leaving, or when you have finished speaking on the phone.

goose A goose is a large bird that has a long neck and webbed feet. Its cry is a loud honking noise.

gooseberry A gooseberry is a small green soft fruit that grows on a bush. It is covered with tiny hairs, and has rather a sharp taste.

gorilla A gorilla is the largest of the apes. It lives in African forests, feeding on fruit and the shoots of young trees. Gorillas live in family groups.

government A government is the group of people in a country or a state who make laws and decide about things that are important, such as medical care and old age pensions.

grab If you grab something you pick it up suddenly and roughly.

gradual Something that is gradual, or happens gradually, happens slowly.

grain
1 Grain is a cereal crop, especially wheat or corn, that has been harvested for food.
2 A grain of something like rice, wheat or other cereal is a seed from it.
3 A grain of something such as sand or salt is a tiny hard piece of it.

gram A gram is a very small unit of weight. One sheet of writing paper weighs about four grams.

granary A granary is a building which is used for storing grain.

grand (grander, grandest)
1 People who are grand seem very important.
2 Buildings that are grand are large and look important.

grape A grape is a small, sweet, round fruit. It can be either pale green or dark purple in colour. Grapes grow in bunches on vines. They can be eaten raw, used for making wine, or dried to make raisins, sultanas or currants.

grapefruit A grapefruit is a large round fruit. It is like an orange, but it is larger and has a pale yellow skin. It has a sharp, slightly bitter taste.

grass is a very common green plant with long thin spiky leaves.

grasshopper A grasshopper is an insect. It has long back legs and can jump well. The male makes a chirping sound by rubbing its back legs against its short leathery wings.

grateful If you are grateful for something nice that someone has done, you have warm friendly feelings towards them and want to thank them.

gravity Gravity is the force which makes things fall to the ground when you drop them, and makes things stay on the ground instead of floating in the air

gravy is a thin sauce made from the juices that come out of meat when you cook it.

graze
1 A graze is a small wound caused by scraping your skin against something.
2 When an animal grazes it eats grass and other plants as they are growing.

grease is a thick oil which is put on the moving parts of cars and other machines to make them work smoothly.

greedy Someone who is greedy is eager for something like money or food. They want more than they need, or more than their fair share.

green
1 A green is an area of land covered with grass, especially in the middle of a town or village.
2 Greens are the green leaves of vegetables such as spinach or cabbage that are cooked and eaten.

greenhouse A greenhouse is a building which has glass walls and roof. It is used to grow plants in.

grief Someone who feels grief is very, very sad, often because a person or animal they love has died.

grip A grip is a firm, strong hold on something.

ground The ground is the surface of the earth or the floor of a room.

group
1 A group is a number of people or things which are together in one place.
2 A group can also mean a set of people who are interested in the same thing, or have something in common.

grow When a person, animal or plant grows, they get bigger.

growl When a dog or other animal growls it makes a low rumbling noise, usually because it is angry.

grub A grub is a young insect which has just come out of an egg.

grunt A grunt is the low rough noise made by pigs.

guard A guard is a person who watches over people, places or objects to keep them safe.

guess A guess is an answer that you give when you do not have all the information you need.

guide
1 A guide is a person who takes people round places such as cities or museums.
2 If you guide someone you show them the right way to go, or show them how to do something.

guilty (guiltier, guiltiest)
1 If someone is guilty of something they have done something wrong.
2 If you feel guilty you feel unhappy because you think you have done something wrong, or have not done something you were supposed to do.

guinea pig A guinea pig is a small furry animal without a tail. Guinea pigs are often kept as pets.

guitar A guitar is a musical instrument made of wood, usually with six strings. You play it by plucking or strumming the strings.

gulf A gulf is a large area of sea which stretches a long way into the land.

gum
1 Your gums are the layers of firm pink flesh inside your mouth. They cover the bone that your teeth are fixed into.
2 Gum is a kind of sweet that you chew but do not swallow.
3 Gum is also a sticky liquid which can be used to fix paper on to something else such as card.
4 A gum is a chewy sweet flavoured so that it tastes like fruit.

gun A gun is a weapon with a long metal tube and a place for bullets. The bullets are forced out of the gun by a small explosion and they fly through the air at great speed.

gunpowder is a mixture which explodes when a flame is put near it. It is used for making things such as fireworks.

gutter A gutter is an open drain for carrying water away. There are gutters on the edges of roofs, and at the side of roads.

habit
1 A habit is something that you do often or regularly, sometimes without thinking about it: *She had a habit of rubbing her ear when she was worried.*
2 If you are in the habit of doing something, you do it often or regularly: *We are in the habit of going camping whenever we can.*

haddock A haddock is a sea fish that you can eat. Haddock are found in the North Atlantic.

hail is small balls of ice that fall like rain from the sky.

hair Your hair is made up of a large number of long, fine threads that grow on your head. Each thread is called a hair. Hair also grows on the bodies of some other animals.

hairy Someone or something that is hairy is covered with hair.

hake is a big fish, similar to cod, that is eaten in Europe and North America.

half
1 If you cut something in half you divide it into two equal parts.
2 A half is a half-price ticket, usually for a child.
3 Half an hour is thirty minutes.
4 You say half past when it is thirty minutes after a particular hour: *It's half past three.*

hall
1 The hall of a house is the area inside the front door that leads to other rooms.
2 A hall is a large room or building that is used for such things as concerts or meetings.
3 The town hall is the place where the local government has its main offices.

ham is meat from the back leg of a pig. It is specially treated so that it can be kept for a long time.

hamburger A hamburger is a piece of minced meat which has been shaped into a flat disc. Hamburgers are fried or grilled and then eaten, often in a bread roll.

hammer
A hammer is a tool that is used for hitting things such as nails into wood.

hamster A hamster is a small furry animal which is often kept as a pet. Hamsters belong to the mouse family. They have very short tails, and large cheek pouches for carrying food.

hand
1 Your hand is the part of your body which is at the end of your arm. It has four fingers and a thumb.
2 If you hand something to someone, you pass it from your hand to theirs.

handbag A handbag is a small bag that women and girls use to hold things such as money and keys.

handkerchief A handkerchief is a small, square piece of fabric that you use for wiping your nose.

handle
1 The handle of a door or window is a small round knob or lever that is used for opening or closing it.
2 The handle of something such as a tool or cup is the part that you hold so that you can pick it up and use it.

handlebars Bicycle handlebars are made from a metal bar. They are fixed to the front of the bicycle and used to steer it.

handsome A man who is handsome has a strong, attractive face.

hang
1 If you hang something up, you fix it there so that it does not touch the ground: *Please hang your coat on the hook.*
2 Something that hangs is heavy or loose so that it swings slightly: *Her long hair hangs over her shoulders.*

hangar A hangar is a large building in which aircraft are kept.

hang-glider A hang-glider is a glider for one person with which they can fly in the air. It is made of fabric stretched over a frame, with a harness underneath.

happen Something that happens takes place as a result of something else.

happiness is the feeling you have when you are happy.

happy Someone who is happy has feelings of pleasure, because something nice has happened or because most things are the way they want.

harbour A harbour is an area of water on a coast which is protected from the open sea by land or strong walls, so that boats can stay there safely.

hard (harder, hardest)
1 An object that is hard is very firm and stiff.
2 If something is hard to do, you cannot do it without a lot of work.

hare A hare is an animal like a rabbit, but larger with long ears and long legs. It does not live in a burrow, but rests in grass or in a ploughed furrow. Hares even have their babies in the open.

harm
1 Harm is injury to a person or animal.
2 To harm something means to damage it.

harness
1 A harness is a set of straps which fit under a person's arms to fasten round their body. It is used to keep a piece of equipment in place, or to hold the person firmly in place.
2 A horse's harness is a set of leather straps fastened round its head or body.

harsh (harsher, harshest)
1 A harsh way of life is very difficult.
2 Weather that is harsh is cold and unpleasant.
3 A person who is harsh is unkind.
4 A voice or other sound that is harsh sounds rough and unpleasant.

harvest The harvest is the cutting or picking of crops when they are ripe.

hat A hat is a head covering for wearing outside. Hats often have a brim round them.

hate
1 If you hate someone or something, you have a very strong feeling of dislike for them.
2 When you say you hate doing something you mean you find it very unpleasant.

hawk A hawk is a large bird with a short, hooked beak, sharp claws, and very good eyesight. Hawks catch and eat small birds and animals.

hay is grass which has been cut and dried to feed animals.

head
1 Your head is the part of your body which has your eyes, nose and mouth in it.
2 Someone who is the head of something such as a company or a school is in charge of it and in charge of the people in it.

health A person's health is how their body is, and whether they are well or ill.

healthy
1 Someone who is healthy is well, and not suffering from any illness.
2 Something that is healthy is good for you and should help you to stay healthy: *You need some healthy outdoor exercise.*

heap
1 A heap of things is a lot of things piled up, usually rather untidily.
2 If someone collapses in a heap, they fall heavily and untidily and do not move.

hear When you hear sounds you notice them by using your ears.

heart Your heart is the organ that pumps the blood round your body.

heat If you heat something you make it warmer, often by using a special piece of equipment: *Heat the milk in a saucepan.*

heavy (heavier, heaviest)
1 Something that is heavy weighs a lot, or weighs more than usual.
2 If a person or an animal has a heavy build, their body is large, solid and strong-looking.

hedge A hedge is a row of bushes or small trees. Hedges can be used to divide two areas of land. They also shelter people and plants from strong winds.

hedgehog A hedgehog is a small brown animal with sharp spikes all over its back. It defends itself by rolling up into a ball.

hedgerow A hedgerow is a row of bushes, trees and plants. Hedgerows usually grow beside country lanes or between fields.

heel
1 Your heel is the back part of your foot.
2 The heel of a shoe is the raised part underneath, at the back.

height
1 The height of a person is how tall they are.
2 The height of an object is its measurement from bottom to top: *A Coast Redwood tree can grow to a height of more than 100 metres.*

helicopter A helicopter is an aircraft without wings. It has one or two sets of large blades which go round above it. It can use the blades to take off straight up into the air, to fly, and to hover.

helmet A helmet is a very hard hat that is worn to protect the head. Hundreds of years ago, knights going into battle wore helmets made of iron or steel.

help
1 If you help someone to do a job, you do part of it for them so that it can be finished more easily or more quickly.
2 If you help someone who is worried or unhappy, you do whatever you can to make them feel better.

helpful People who are helpful do whatever they can to make things easier for other people.

hem The hem of a garment is the bottom edge of it. It is folded over and sewn to make it neat.

hen
1 A hen is a female chicken. Some people keep hens for their eggs.
2 A hen can also be any female bird.

herd A herd is a large group of animals of one kind that live together.

here You say here when you mean the place where you are: *I'll stand here and wait.*

heron A heron is a wading bird which has very long legs, a long beak and grey and black feathers.

herring A herring is a long silver-coloured fish that lives in large groups in the sea. Herrings are caught as food.

hexagon A hexagon is a shape that has six straight sides.

hidden Something that is hidden is not easily noticed.

hide If you hide somewhere, you go where you cannot easily be seen.

high Something that is high is a long way from the bottom to the top: *The wall round the garden is quite high.*

hill A hill is an area of land that is higher than the land around it. A hill is not as high as a mountain.

hinge Hinges are pieces of metal, wood or plastic that are used to hold a door so that it can swing freely.

hippopotamus A hippopotamus is a large African animal with short legs. It has thick wrinkled skin without any fur. Hippopotamuses live in herds on the banks of large rivers. They spend a lot of time in the water.

history is the story of things that have happened in the past.

hit If you hit a ball you make it move by touching it hard with something like a bat.

hobby A hobby is something you enjoy doing in your spare time, such as collecting stamps or birdwatching.

hockey is an outdoor game, played between teams of 11 players. They use long curved sticks to hit a small ball, and they try to score goals.

hollow
1 A hollow is an area that is lower than the ground around it.
2 Something that is hollow has a space inside it: *The owl lived in a hollow tree trunk.*

home
1 Your home is the place where you live and feel you belong.
2 If you feel at home somewhere, you feel comfortable and like being there.
3 A home game is one that is played on your team's own ground.

honest (say onnest) Someone who is honest tells the truth and can be trusted.

honey Honey is a sweet, sticky, golden liquid that is made by bees. People often eat honey spread on bread.

honeycomb A honeycomb is the place inside a hive where the honey is stored. It has lots of six-sided holes made by worker bees from wax.

hood
1 A hood is part of a garment such as a coat or cloak, which you can pull up to cover your head.
2 A hood is also a covering on a vehicle. It is usually made of strong fabric fixed to metal strips so that it can be raised or lowered: *It began to rain, so she put the hood up on the pram.*

hoof The hoof of an animal such as a horse is the hard, bony part of its foot.

hook
1 A hook is a bent piece of something like metal or plastic that is used for holding things, or hanging things up.
2 A hook made for fishing is a bent piece of thin metal.

hop
1 If you hop, you move in small jumps using only one foot.
2 When birds and some small animals hop, they move in small jumps using both feet together.

hope is a feeling that you want things to go well in the future, and believe that they will.

horizon The horizon is the line in the far distance where the sky seems to touch the land or the sea.

horizontal Something that is horizontal is flat and parallel with the ground.

horn
1 Horns are the hard, pointed growths that stick out of the top of the head of animals such as goats and bulls.
2 A horn is an object that is built into vehicles such as cars. It makes a loud noise as a signal or warning.

horrible Something that is horrible is awful or very unpleasant.

horror is a very strong feeling of fear or shock. It is caused by something you find very, very unpleasant.

horse A horse is a large animal which people ride for pleasure, or to get from one place to another. Horses are also used for pulling things such as ploughs and carts.

horseshoe A horseshoe is a piece of metal shaped like a U. It is fixed with nails to the underneath of a horse's hoof. This does not hurt the horse.

hospital A hospital is a place where people who are ill or injured are looked after by doctors and nurses.

hot (hotter, hottest)
1 Something that is hot has a high temperature.
2 If you are hot, you feel too warm to be comfortable.

hot dog A hot dog is a long bread roll with a sausage inside.

hotel A hotel is a building where people pay to stay, usually for a few nights.

hour An hour is a period of 60 minutes. There are 24 hours in a day.

house A house is a building where people live.

hover To hover means to stay in one place in the air. Many birds and insects can hover by moving their wings very quickly.

hovercraft A hovercraft is a vehicle that glides over water or land on a cushion of air.

howl
1 If an animal such as a dog or a wolf howls, it makes a long, loud, wailing sound.
2 When the wind howls it makes a wailing noise, usually because it is blowing through a narrow gap.

hug When you hug someone you put your arms around them tightly because you like them.

huge Something that is huge is very, very big.

human being A human being is a man, woman or child.

humble (humbler, humblest) Someone who is humble feels that they are not important.

hungry (hungrier, hungriest) When you are hungry you want to eat, because your stomach is empty.

hunt
1 When people or animals hunt, they chase wild animals to kill them, usually for food.
2 If you hunt for something, you try to find it by looking carefully.

hurricane A hurricane is a very violent wind or storm.

hurry
1 If you hurry somewhere you go as quickly as you can.
2 If you hurry to do something you do it faster than usual.

hurt
1 When part of your body hurts, you feel pain.
2 If you have been hurt, you have been injured.

hut A hut is a small house with only one or two rooms.

hutch A hutch is a cage made of wood and wire netting. Pets such as rabbits are kept in hutches.

hyena A hyena is an animal that looks like a wolf. It has very strong jaws and neck, but quite small back legs. Hyenas live in Africa and parts of Asia. They make a sound rather like a human's laugh.

ice is water that has frozen and become solid.

iceberg An iceberg is a huge block of ice floating in the sea. Only the top of an iceberg shows. Most of it is under water

ice cream is a very cold, sweet-tasting, creamy food.

icicle An icicle is a piece of ice shaped like a pointed stick. Icicles hang from roofs, or wherever water has been dripping and freezing.

icing is a mixture of powdered sugar and water or egg whites. It is used to cover cakes as a decoration.

idea If you have an idea, you suddenly think of a way of doing something.

idle
1 An idle person is someone who does not do very much, even if there is plenty to do.
2 Machines or factories that are idle are not being used.

ill Someone who is ill has something wrong with their health: *She felt ill and had to go home to bed.*

imaginary Something that is imaginary is not real. It is only in your mind: *She liked to have imaginary talks with famous people.*

imagine When you imagine something, you think about it and form a picture of it in your mind.

imitate If you imitate a person or animal, you copy the way they speak or behave.

immediately If you do something immediately, you do it without doing anything else in between: *I must go to London immediately. I won't stop for lunch.*

impatient Someone who is impatient does not like to be kept waiting for anything. They get annoyed if they think people are doing things too slowly.

important If someone says something is important, they mean it matters a lot: *It is important to protect animals that are in danger of extinction.*

impossible Something that is impossible cannot be done.

improve If something improves it gets better.

indoors When you are indoors, you are inside a building.

infant An infant is a baby or a very young child.

information If someone gives you information about something, they tell you about it: *For information on books for young readers, ask at your library.*

inhabitant The inhabitants of a place are the people or animals that live there.

injure If a person or animal is injured, part of their body is damaged.

injury If a person or an animal has an injury, part of their body has been damaged.

ink is the coloured liquid that is used for writing and printing.

inn An inn is a small, old hotel, usually in the country, where people can pay for food and somewhere to sleep. Inns often have a bar where people can buy drinks.

insect An insect is a small animal that has six legs. Most insects have wings. Ants, flies, butterflies and beetles are all insects.

instead means in place of something else: *I don't want to go to the fair. I'd rather play trains instead.*

instrument
1 An instrument is a kind of tool that is used to do a particular job: *The dentist had a tray of instruments in front of him.*
2 Instruments are also things that are used to measure something such as speed, or height above the ground. Drivers and pilots use instruments like these in their vehicles.
3 A musical instrument is something such as a piano, guitar or violin that you play to make music.

intelligent
1 A person who is intelligent can understand, learn, and think things out quickly and well.
2 An animal that is intelligent shows that it can think and understand.

interest If something interests you, you want to find out more about it.

interesting If you find something interesting, it attracts your attention. This could be because you think it is rather exciting or unusual.

interfere If something interferes with something else, it gets in the way: *You shouldn't watch so much television. It interferes with your homework.*

jam is a food that is made by cooking fruit with a lot of sugar.

January is the first month of the year. It has 31 days.

jar A jar is a container. It is usually shaped like a cylinder and is made of glass. Jars are used for storing food such as jam or preserved fruit.

jaw Your jaw is the lower part of your face below your mouth. It moves up and down when you eat or talk.

jealous (say jellus) Someone who is jealous feels upset because something they think belongs to them is being given to someone else: *He felt jealous of the new baby, because suddenly everyone was playing with it instead of talking to him.*

jeans are trousers that are usually made from a strong cotton cloth.

jelly is clear food that wobbles when you move it. You can eat it as a cold pudding.

jellyfish A jellyfish is a creature that lives in the sea. It has an umbrella-shaped body that looks like clear jelly.

jerk If something happens with a jerk, it happens suddenly with a quick movement.

jet
1 A jet is an aircraft with special engines. It can fly very fast and high up.
2 A jet of something such as water is a thin, forceful stream of it.

jewel A jewel is a precious stone such as a diamond or a ruby. Jewels are often used to make things such as rings and necklaces.

jewellery is the name for ornaments such as rings or necklaces that people can wear. Jewellery is often made of valuable metal such as gold or silver. It is sometimes decorated with precious stones.

jigsaw A jigsaw is a game which uses a picture cut into a lot of pieces. You have to put the picture back together again by finding the right place for all the pieces.

job
1 A job is the work that someone does to earn money.
2 A job can also be anything that has to be done: *There are always plenty of jobs to do when I get home.*

join
1 If you join two things you fix them together.
2 If you join something like a club, you become a member of it.

joint
1 A joint is a part of your body such as your elbow or knee, where two bones meet and are able to move.
2 A joint is any place where two things are fastened together.

joke A joke is something that is done or said to make you laugh.

journey If you go on a journey, you travel from one place to another.

jug A jug is a container shaped like a cylinder. It has a handle and a spout.

juice Juice is the liquid that comes from fruit such as oranges when you squeeze them.

juicy (juicier, juiciest) Something that is juicy has a lot of juice in it and is very enjoyable to eat.

July is the seventh month of the year. It has 31 days.

jump
1 When you jump you move quickly and suddenly up in the air, using your own strength.
2 If you jump when something startles you, you make a sudden sharp movement.

jumper A jumper is a piece of clothing, usually made of wool, that covers the top part of your body. It has long sleeves and does not open at the front.

junction A junction is a place where roads or railway lines meet.

June is the sixth month of the year. It has 30 days.

jungle A jungle is a forest in a hot country. There are a very large number of tall trees and other plants growing closely together.

junior Someone who is junior in something like a company or the government is less important than other people who work there.

junk
1 A junk is a Chinese sailing boat that has a flat bottom and square sails.
2 Junk is old and second-hand things that are being sold cheaply: *We bought most of our furniture at junk shops.*

kangaroo A kangaroo is a large Australian animal which moves forward by jumping on its back legs. Female kangaroos carry their babies in a special pouch on their stomachs.

keep
1 If you keep something for somebody you save it for them: *Can I keep this piece of cake for my brother?*
2 If you keep doing something, you do it over and over again: *She will keep leaving the door open.*

kennel A kennel is a small building made for a dog to sleep in.

kerb A kerb is the edge of a pavement.

kettle A kettle is a covered container made of metal. It has a handle on the top and a spout at the side. It is used for boiling water.

key
1 A key is a specially shaped piece of metal that you use for locking things such as doors and padlocks.
2 The keys on a piece of equipment such as a typewriter or a piano are the parts that you press to make it work.

kick If you kick something you hit it hard with your foot.

kill To kill someone or something means to cause them to die.

kilogram A kilogram is a measure of weight. It is called a kilo for short. It is equal to 1000 grams.

kilometre A kilometre is a measure of distance. It is equal to 1000 metres.

kilt A kilt is a pleated skirt worn as part of the national costume of Scotland. It is made of woollen material woven in a special squared pattern called tartan.

kind
1 Someone who is kind behaves in a gentle, caring way.
2 If you talk about a kind of object, you mean that sort of object: *I want that kind of pen, please. The red one.*

kindness is when someone is being friendly and helpful towards someone else.

king A king is a man who rules a country. Kings are not chosen by the people, but are born into a royal family. The eldest son of the king becomes king when his father dies.

kingfisher A kingfisher is a brightly-coloured bird that lives by the banks of rivers.

kiss If you kiss someone you touch them lightly with your lips as a sign of affection.

kit

1 A kit is a set of things that are used for a particular purpose: *Have you seen my first aid kit?*

2 A kit is also a set of parts that can be put together to make something: *I'd like a model aircraft kit for my birthday.*

kitchen A kitchen is a room that is used for cooking and washing up.

kite A kite is an object made from a light frame covered with paper or cloth. It has a long string fixed to it.

kitten A kitten is a very young cat.

kiwi A kiwi is a bird that lives in New Zealand. Kiwis cannot fly, but they can run fast. They are nocturnal.

kiwi fruit A kiwi fruit is the oval fruit of the kiwi plant. It has a brown furry skin and pale green flesh. It is also called a Chinese gooseberry.

knee Your knee is the joint where your leg bends.

knife A knife is an object that you use for cutting. You hold it in your hand. It is made from a sharp, flat piece of metal which is fixed into a handle.

knight

1 Hundreds of years ago, a knight was a man who fought battles for his king. He rode a horse and wore armour.

2 Now, a knight is a man who is allowed to put 'Sir' in front of his name.

3 In chess, a knight is a piece which is shaped like a horse's head.

knit If you knit, you make something such as a jumper from wool or a similar thread.

knob

1 A knob is a round handle on a door or a drawer.

2 A knob is also a round button on a piece of equipment such as a radio.

knock

1 If you knock at a door, you hit it so that someone will hear and open the door to you.

2 If you knock something over, you touch it roughly, usually by accident, and it falls over.

knot

1 A knot is the place where a piece of something such as string or cloth is tied.

2 A knot in a piece of wood is a small hard area where a branch once grew.

3 A knot is also a measure of speed for ships.

know If you know something, you have it in your mind and you are sure it is true.

knowledge is what people know about things.

knuckle Your knuckles are the rounded pieces of bone where your fingers join your hands. Sometimes the bony places where your fingers bend are also called knuckles.

koala A koala is an Australian animal. It looks like a small bear with grey fur and tufted ears. Koalas live in trees and eat leaves.

kookaburra A kookaburra is a large Australian kingfisher. This bird has a strange cry like a human laugh. It is also known as a laughing jackass.

label A label is a piece of paper or cloth that is fixed to an object. The label tells you things about the object. For example, the label on a medicine bottle tells you what the medicine is called and how you should take it.

laboratory A laboratory is a building or a room that contains special equipment. Scientists use laboratories for their work.

lace is an ornamental fabric with a lot of holes in it. It is made by looping or twisting fine threads.

laces are pieces of cord that are put through holes along two edges of something. The laces are pulled tight and tied, to fasten the two edges together.

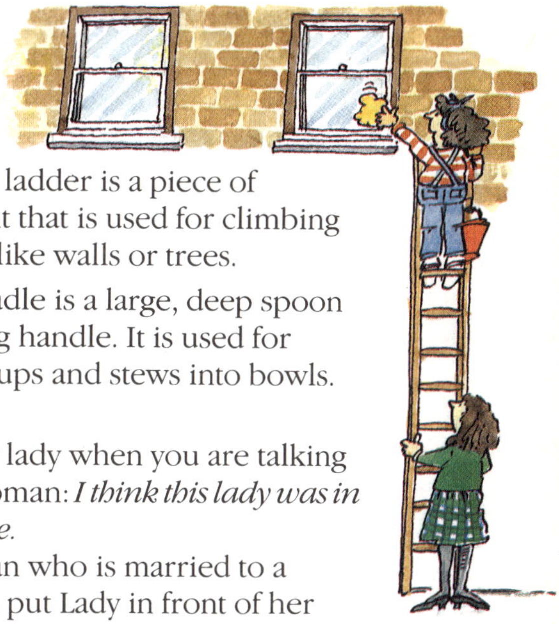

ladder A ladder is a piece of equipment that is used for climbing up things like walls or trees.

ladle A ladle is a large, deep spoon with a long handle. It is used for putting soups and stews into bowls.

lady
1 You say lady when you are talking about a woman: *I think this lady was in front of me.*
2 A woman who is married to a knight can put Lady in front of her name: Sir John and Lady Brown.

ladybird A ladybird is a small round beetle with spots on its wings. Ladybirds are usually orangey-red, with black spots.

lake A lake is a large area of fresh water with land all round it.

lamp A lamp is an object that gives light by burning oil or gas, or by using electricity.

lance A lance is a long spear that used to be carried by soldiers on horseback.

land
1 Land is the part of the world that is solid, dry ground. It is not covered by sea.
2 If something such as an aircraft lands, it comes down from the air on to land or water.

lane
1 A lane is a narrow road, especially in the country.
2 A lane is also part of a main road or motorway. It is marked with lines to show drivers where to go.

language is the words that are used by people when they speak or write.

lantern A lantern is a kind of lamp. It has a metal frame with glass sides. Lanterns usually hold oil, and have a special piece of string inside called a wick. When the wick is lit, it burns the oil slowly to give a light.

lard is soft, white, animal fat which is used for cooking.

larder A larder is a room or a cupboard in a house, where food is kept.

large (larger, largest) Something that is large is bigger than others of its kind: *They saw some large ants running amongst the others.*

lark A lark is a small brown bird with a sweet song. The male circles high above the ground as he sings.

larva A larva is an insect at an early stage of its life. It looks like a short, fat worm.

lasso A lasso is a long rope with a sliding loop at one end. Cowboys use lassoes to catch cattle and horses.

late (later, latest)
1 You say late when you mean after your usual bedtime: *Can I stay up late this evening?*
2 If you are late arriving somewhere, you get there after the time you were supposed to: *I was late for school this morning.*

laugh (say larf) When you laugh, you make the sound people make when they are happy or when they think something is very funny.

launch When something such as a rocket or satellite is launched, it is sent into the air or into space.

launderette A launderette is a shop where there are washing machines and driers. People can pay to use the machines to wash and dry their clothes.

lava is a kind of rock. It comes out of volcanoes as a very hot liquid. Then it cools and becomes solid.

lavatory
1 A lavatory is the same as a toilet. It is a deep bowl which is joined to a drain. It has a seat on top with a large hole in the middle.
2 A lavatory is also the room where the lavatory is. Sometimes there is a washbasin in the room as well.

law A law is a rule that is made by a government.

lawn A lawn is an area of grass that is kept short. It is usually part of someone's garden.

lay
1 If you lay something somewhere, you put it there carefully.
2 If you lay the table, you put things like knives and forks on the table ready for a meal.

layer A layer is a single thickness of something that lies on top of or underneath something else.

lazy Someone who is lazy does not want to work or do anything hard.

lead (as in feed)
1 A dog's lead is a long, thin piece of leather or a chain. You fix one end of it to the dog's collar and hold the other end.
2 Someone who leads a group of people is in charge of them.
3 If you lead someone to a particular place you go with them to show them where it is.

lead (as in fed)
1 Lead is a grey, heavy metal.
2 The lead in a pencil is the centre part of it that makes a mark on paper.

leaf
1 A leaf is one of the thin, flat parts of a plant. Leaves are usually green. Different sorts of plant have differently shaped leaves.
2 A leaf is also one of the pieces of paper in a book.
3 The leaf of a table is a part of the top that can be folded or slid out of the way when it is not needed.

leak If something such as water leaks, it gets through a hole that should not be there.

leap If you leap somewhere, you jump a long way.

learn When you learn something, you get to know it, or find out how to do it: *She soon learned to read.*

leather Leather is the specially treated skin of animals. It is used for making things such as shoes or furniture.

leek A leek is a long, thin vegetable. It is white at the root end, and has long green leaves. It is used in cooking and tastes rather like an onion.

left is the side of the page that you begin reading on in English.

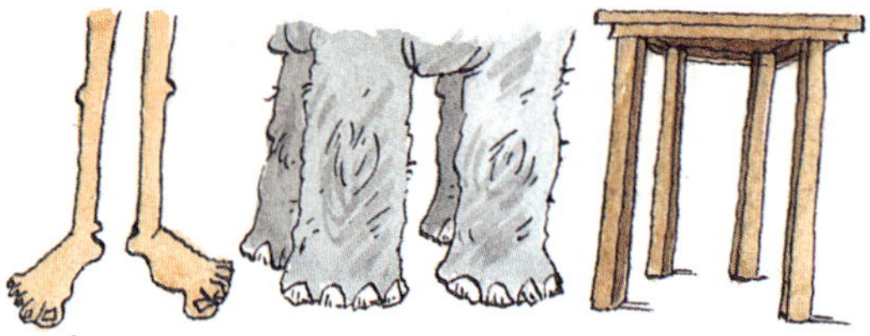

leg
1 Your legs are the two long parts of your body that you use for walking.
2 The legs of an animal are the thin parts of its body that it uses for standing and moving.
3 The legs of a piece of furniture such as a table or chair are the parts that rest on the floor and support the main part.

lemon A lemon is an oval-shaped fruit. It has a thick yellow skin. Lemons are juicy, but they taste sour.

lemonade is a drink that is made from lemon, sugar and water.

lend If you lend something to someone, you let them have something of yours for a while: *Could you lend me your pencil, please?*

length
1 The length of something is the distance that it measures from one end to the other.
2 The length of something such as a holiday is the period of time that it lasts.

lens A lens is a thin piece of clear material such as glass. It has a curved surface which makes things look clearer, larger, or smaller. Lenses are used in spectacles, cameras and microscopes.

leopard A leopard is a member of the cat family. It lives in the forests of Africa and Asia. Its coat is yellow with black spots in the shape of circles. Leopards are about two metres long, from nose to tip of tail.

less means not as much as something else: *A shower uses less water than a bath.*

letter
1 A letter is a message that is written down on paper. You usually put a letter in an envelope and post it.
2 A letter is also a written symbol which stands for one of the sounds in a language: *She went for an eye test and was asked to read the letters on the card.*

lettuce A lettuce is a plant with large green leaves. You can eat it raw in salads.

level Something that is level is completely flat with no part higher than any other part.

lever
1 A lever is a long handle that is fixed to a piece of machinery. The lever is pulled or pushed to make the machine work.
2 A lever is also a long bar which can help lift heavy weights.

library A library is a place where they keep books and newspapers. Many libraries allow people to borrow books for certain periods.

lick If you lick something, you move your tongue across it: *She licked her ice cream.*

lid A lid is the top of a box or other container. It can be raised or taken off when you want to open the container.

lie
1 A lie is something that someone says which they know is not true.
2 If you lie somewhere your body is flat on the ground or on a bed of some kind.

life is being alive. All living things – humans, animals and plants – have life.

lifeboat
1 A lifeboat is a medium-sized boat which is sent out to sea to rescue people in danger.
2 A lifeboat is also a small boat which is carried on a ship. If the ship is in danger of sinking, people can use the lifeboat to escape.

lift
1 A lift is something like a small room that moves up and down inside a tall building.
2 If you lift something, you take it in your hands and move it upwards.
3 If you lift your eyes or your head, you look up.

light
1 Light is the thing that lets you see. It comes from the sun and moon, and from things such as lamps and torches.
2 A light is anything that makes light.
3 If you light something you make it start burning: *They decided to light the fire.*
4 Something that is light to carry does not weigh very much.
5 Light colours are very pale.
6 Light winds blow gently.

lighthouse A lighthouse is a tower containing a powerful flashing light. Lighthouses are built on the coast or on small islands in the sea. They are used to guide ships or to warn them of danger.

lightning is a very bright flash of light in the sky that happens during a thunderstorm.

lilac A lilac is a small tree which has sweet-smelling flowers. The flowers grow tightly together in large, cone-shaped groups.

limb
1 Your limbs are your arms and legs.
2 The limbs of a tree are its branches.

lime
1 A lime is a small round fruit. It has a dark green skin, and tastes like a lemon.
2 A lime is also a large tree with pale green leaves.

limp (limper, limpest)
1 If a person or animal limps, they walk unevenly. They usually limp because there is something wrong with one foot or leg.
2 If someone is limp they have no strength or energy.
3 Something that is limp is soft and not crisp or firm: *I'm going to throw this lettuce away – it's gone limp.*

limpet A limpet is a small sea animal. It has a cone-shaped shell. Limpets fix themselves tightly to rocks.

line
1 A line is a long thin mark on a surface. Some writing paper has lines on it to show you where to write.
2 A line of people or things is a number of them in a row.

lion A lion is a large animal of the cat family. Lions live in parts of Africa and Asia, in groups called prides.

lip Your lips are the top and bottom outer edges of your mouth.

liquid A liquid is something like water which is not solid and can be poured.

list A list is a set of things that are written down one below the other.

listen If you listen to a sound that you can hear, you give it your attention: *Please listen when I'm talking to you.*

litre A litre is a measurement of the amount of space that something takes up. Liquids such as orange juice and wine are sold in litres.

litter
1 Litter is rubbish such as bits of paper and bottles that are left lying untidily outside.
2 A litter is a group of animals born to the same mother at the same time.

live (as in give)
1 To live means to be alive.
2 If someone lives in a particular place, that is where their home is.

live (as in five) Live animals or plants are alive.

lively (livelier, liveliest)
1 Someone who is lively is cheerful and full of energy.
2 A place that is lively has a lot of interesting and exciting things happening.

liver Your liver is a large organ in your body. Its job is to clean your blood.

living
1 Living things are things which can have life. Humans, animals and plants are all living things.
2 Someone who is living is alive now.

living room The living room in a house is the room where the family spend most of their time.

lizard A lizard is a small animal with four short legs and a long tail. It has a rough dry skin. Lizards are reptiles. Their babies hatch from eggs.

llama A llama is a South American animal of the camel family. It has thick long hair. Llamas are used by humans to carry things. People also eat the flesh of llamas, and use their wool for clothing.

load
1 A load is things which are being carried somewhere.
2 If someone loads a vehicle they put things in it to be taken somewhere.

loaf A loaf of bread is bread that has been baked in a special shape. You can cut loaves into slices.

loch A loch is the Scottish name for a lake.

lock A lock is an object which is used to keep something such as a door or a case shut. Only a person with a key can open a lock.

locomotive A locomotive is a railway engine driven by steam, electricity or diesel power. It is used to pull trains along railway tracks.

locust A locust is an insect that belongs to the same family as a grasshopper. It has long legs and wings. It lives mainly in hot countries. Locusts fly in large groups called swarms. They cause great damage by eating crops.

loft A loft is the space inside the sloping roof of a house or other building. People sometimes store things in lofts.

log
1 A log is a piece of a thick branch from a tree.
2 A log is also a record of things that happen, especially on a ship or aircraft.

lollipop A lollipop is a large round sweet on a stick.

lonely
1 Someone who is lonely is unhappy because they do not have any friends, or do not have anyone to talk to.
2 A lonely place is a place that not many people go to.

look If you look in a particular direction, you direct your eyes that way so that you can see what is there.

loom
1 A loom is a machine that is used for weaving thread into cloth.
2 If something looms, it appears as a tall, unclear shape, often in a frightening way: *The trees loomed above him in the fog.*

loop A loop is a circular shape in something long and thin. When you tie shoelaces, the bow has two loops.

loose (looser, loosest) Something that is lose is not firmly fixed in place: *I have a loose tooth.*

lord
1 Hundreds of years ago, a lord was a man who owned large areas of land and a lot of buildings. He had power over many other people. People worked for him, and in exchange he protected them.
2 Now, Lord is a title which is put in front of some important people's names in Britain.

lorry A lorry is a large vehicle that is used to carry loads by road.

lose
1 If you lose something, you do not know where it is.

2 If someone loses weight, they become thinner.
3 If a clock or watch loses time, it goes slower than it should do.

lost
1 If you are lost, you cannot find your way or do not know where you are.
2 If something is lost, you cannot find it.

loud (louder, loudest) A loud sound is one that makes a lot of noise and is easy to hear.

loudspeaker A loudspeaker is a piece of equipment that is used so that sounds can be heard. Microphones, radios and record players all need loudspeakers.

lounge A lounge is a room in a house or hotel where people sit and relax.

love
1 Love is a very strong feeling of affection for someone.
2 If you love someone, you like them very, very much and they are very important to you.

lovely (lovelier, loveliest) Something that is lovely is very pleasing to look at or listen to.

low (lower, lowest)
1 Something that is low measures only a short distance from the ground to the top: *There was a low wall that they used to jump over.*
2 If the sun or moon is low, it is close to the horizon.
3 If a river is low, there is less water in it than usual.
4 If the price of something is low, it is cheaper than usual.
5 If an amount of something is low, there is less than there needs to be: *We're getting very low on reading books.*
6 An oven that is turned down low is set so that it does not give much heat.
7 Someone who is feeling low feels rather miserable.

lower
1 Lower means something that is below something else: *Tom wanted to sleep on the lower bunk.*
2 If you lower something you move it slowly downwards: *As it was getting dark, she lowered the blind.*
3 If you lower your voice, you speak more quietly.

loyal Someone who is loyal stays firm in their friendship for someone.

luck is something that seems to happen without any reason. Luck can be good or bad: *It was really bad luck - I broke my leg the day before we were going on holiday.*

lucky Someone who is lucky seems to have good luck.

luggage is made up of the suitcases, bags and things that you take with you when you are travelling.

lump
1 A lump is a piece of something solid: *She took a lump of modelling clay and started to make an animal.*
2 A lump on someone's body is a small swelling.
3 A lump of sugar is a small amount of it, shaped like a cube.

lunar If someone says lunar they are talking about the moon.

lunch is a meal that you have in the middle of the day.

lungs Your lungs are the two parts of your body inside your chest that fill with air when you breathe.

lynx A lynx is a very keen-sighted animal of the cat family. Lynxes live in rocky places and forests. They can climb well and spend a lot of time in the branches of trees.

machine A machine is a piece of equipment which does a particular kind of work. It is usually powered by an engine or by electricity.

magazine A magazine is a thin book which comes out regularly, usually once a week or once a month. It has articles, stories and pictures.

magic In fairy stories, magic is the thing that makes impossible things happen: *The fairy used her magic to turn the frog into a prince.*

male A male is a person or animal that can become a father.

mammal A mammal is a warm-blooded animal. Female mammals do not lay eggs. They feed their babies with milk from their own bodies. Human beings, cats and whales are all mammals.

man
1 A man is an adult male human.
2 You can say man to mean human beings in general: *Man is a mammal that walks on two legs.*

mane The mane of an animal such as a horse or a lion is the long thick hair that grows from its neck.

map A map is a drawing of a particular area as it would look from above.

maple A maple is a tree with five-pointed leaves. Maples grow in cool areas.

marble
1 Marble is a type of very hard rock. It shines when it is polished. Statues and parts of buildings are sometimes made of marble.
2 A marble is one of the small, coloured glass balls used by children in the game of marbles.

March March is the third month of the year. It has 31 days.

march
1 A march is a piece of music. It has a regular rhythm that you can march to.
2 If you march, you walk with regular steps, like a soldier.

margarine is a soft, yellow mixture that looks like butter. It is made with vegetable oil. You can spread it on bread or use it in cooking.

mark
1 A mark is a small part of a surface which is a different colour because something has been dropped on it, or because it has been damaged in some way: *Your shirt has got a dirty mark on it.*
2 A mark is also something which has been written or drawn: *He made a lot of little marks on the paper with his pencil.*
3 Teachers sometimes give marks to show how good or bad a student's work is.

market A market is a place where things are bought and sold. Markets are often held somewhere outside such as in the centre of a town. In some towns markets are held regularly, for example once a week.

marmalade is a food rather like jam. It is made from fruit such as oranges or lemons. It is usually eaten for breakfast, spread on bread or toast.

marry A man and a woman who marry become husband and wife.

marsh A marsh is an area of land which is always very wet and muddy. This is usually because water cannot drain from it properly.

marsupial A marsupial is an animal whose babies are carried in a pouch at the front of their mother's body. Kangaroos and opossums are marsupials.

marvellous Something that is marvellous is wonderful, and even better than you expected.

mask A mask is something that you wear over your face. There are usually holes that you can see through. Some masks are funny, and some are frightening.

mast A mast is a long vertical pole on a sailing ship. It is used to hold the sails and flags.

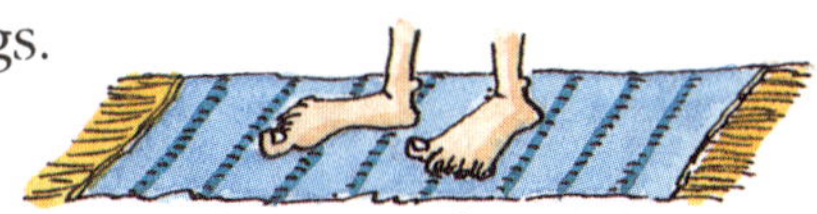

mat A mat is a small piece of carpet or other material that is put on the floor.

match
1 A match is an organized game of something like tennis or football.
2 A match is also a small thin stick of wood or card. One end is specially treated so that when you brush it hard against a matchbox it makes a flame.

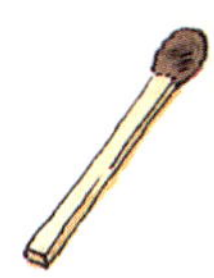

3 If you match one thing with another, you decide there is some connection between them. In some tests or puzzles you are asked to match things from a list: *Can you match the animals with the countries they come from?*

material
1 A material is anything solid that can be used to make something else. Wood, iron and stone are all materials.
2 Material is fabric that you can use to make things like clothes and curtains.

mathematics is the study of numbers, quantities and shapes. Arithmetic is part of mathematics.

matron A matron is the most senior nurse in a hospital.

matter Matter is what the world is made of. Solids, liquids and gases are all matter.

mattress A mattress is a large, flat cushion which is the same size as a bed. It is put on a bed to make it comfortable to lie on.

May is the fifth month of the year. It has 31 days.

may
1 When you say that something may be true, you mean it could be true but you are not sure.
2 If someone says you may do something, you are allowed to do it.

mayor The mayor of a town or city is the man or woman who has been chosen to be its head for one year.

meadow (say meddo) a meadow is a field of grass and flowers.

meal A meal is food that people eat, usually at set times during the day.

mean (meaner, meanest)
1 If you ask what something means, you want it explained to you.
2 Someone who is mean is too careful with something such as money.

means The means of doing something is the way it is done: *The car has broken down. We shall have to find some other means of getting there.*

measles is an illness. It gives you a high temperature and red spots on your skin.

measure If you measure something, you find out how large or heavy it is: *Use your ruler to measure this table.*

meat Meat is flesh taken from an animal that has been killed for eating.

medal A medal is a small piece of metal in the shape of a circle or a cross. It is given for bravery, or as a prize.

medicine is something that is given to a person who is ill.

meet If you meet someone, you go to the same place at the same time as they do.

melon A melon is a large fruit which is sweet and juicy inside. It has a thick, hard green or yellow skin.

melt When something melts it changes from a solid into a liquid.

member A member of a group is one of the people, animals or things belonging to that group: *A lion is a member of the cat family.*

memory
1 Your memory is your ability to remember things: *If you want to be an actor you need a good memory.*
2 A memory is something you remember from the past: *The memory of the holiday was still fresh in her mind.*

mend If you mend something that is broken or does not work, you put it right so that it can be used again.

mercury is a silver-coloured metal. It is usually in liquid form. It is used in thermometers to measure temperature.

mess If you say something is a mess, you mean it is very untidy.

message A message is words that you send or leave when you cannot speak directly to someone.

metal is a hard material such as iron, steel or copper. Metals are used for making things like tools or machinery.

meteor A meteor is a piece of rock or metal that shoots across the sky. It burns very brightly as it enters the earth's atmosphere.

meter A meter is an instrument for measuring something such as the amount of gas or electricity you have used.

metre A metre is a measure of length. It is equal to 100 centimetres.

microphone A microphone is an instrument that you speak into when you want to make your voice louder. You also need a microphone if you want to record what you are saying.

microscope A microscope is an instrument which helps you to see very tiny things. You look at things through a special lens which makes them seem much bigger.

microwave A microwave oven is one which cooks food very quickly.

midday is 12 o'clock in the middle of the day.

middle The middle object or person in a row is the one that has an equal number on each side: *I'm in the middle of this row. I've got two people on one side and two people on the other.*

midnight Midnight is 12 o'clock in the middle of the night.

might
1 Might is power or strength: *He struggled with all his might to lift the heavy case.*
2 If you say something might happen, you mean you are not sure if it will.

mild (milder, mildest)
1 If someone is mild, they are gentle and kind.
2 Mild weather is warmer than usual for the time of year.
3 Mild soap will not damage the things you want to wash.

mile A mile is a measure of distance. It is equal to 1.6 kilometres.

milk is the white liquid that female mammals make in their bodies to feed their young.

mill
1 A mill is a building in which grain is crushed to make flour.
2 A mill is also a factory used for making a particular material such as wool, cotton or steel.

million A million is a thousand thousands. In figures, it is written 1,000,000.

mince
1 Mince is beef which has been put through a special machine. The machine cuts it into very small pieces.
2 If you mince meat, you cut it into very small pieces.

mincemeat is a sticky mixture of dried fruit and other sweet things. Mincemeat is usually cooked in pastry to make mince pies.

mind
1 Your mind is where your thoughts are.
2 If you tell someone to mind something, you are warning them to be careful: *Mind your head.*
3 If you mind something or somebody, you look after them for a while: *Could you mind the baby while I have a rest?*

mine A mine is a place where people dig deep holes to find something like coal or diamonds.

mineral A mineral is a material that is formed naturally in rocks and the earth. Tin, salt and sulphur are minerals.

minister
1 A minister is an important member of the government of a country.
2 A minister is also a person who is in charge of a church.

minor
1 A minor is a person who is not yet adult. In Britain, anyone under the age of 18 is a minor.
2 Something that is minor is not very important or serious.

mint
1 Mint is a small plant. Its leaves have a strong taste and smell. Mint is used in cooking.
2 A mint is the place where the coins of a country are made.

minute (say minnit) A minute is a measure of time. There are 60 minutes to an hour.

minute (say mynewt) Something that is minute is very, very small.

miracle A miracle is something wonderful and surprising that cannot be explained.

mirror A mirror is a flat piece of glass that reflects light. When you look in a mirror, you can see yourself.

mischief is silly things that some children do to annoy other people.

miserable Someone who is miserable is very unhappy.

misery Misery is great unhappiness.

miss
1 If you miss something you do not notice it: *We missed our turning and had to go back.*
2 If you are aiming at something and miss, you fail to hit it.
3 If you miss a bus or train, you are too late to get on it.
4 If you miss somebody you are lonely without them.

missile
1 A missile is a weapon like a rocket.
2 A missile is also any object that is thrown at someone.

mist A mist is a large number of tiny drops of water in the air. When there is a mist you cannot see very far.

mistake A mistake is something which is not quite right: *There are two spelling mistakes on that page.*

mix If you mix two things you stir them or put them together in some way. Then they become one thing: *The children made paste by mixing flour and water.*

mixture A mixture is something that is made by mixing two or more things. A mixture is usually a liquid or a rather sticky solid.

moan A moan is a low, miserable cry. People moan if they are in pain or are very unhappy.

moist (moister, moistest) Something that is moist is slightly wet.

moisture Moisture is tiny drops of water in the air or on a surface.

mole
1 A mole is a small dark lump on someone's skin.
2 A mole is also a small animal. It has tiny eyes and short, dark, silky fur. Moles have strong front claws and are very good at digging. They live most of the time on their own in tunnels in the ground. Moles eat insects and worms.

moment A moment is a very short period of time.

monastery A monastery is a place where monks live and work.

Monday Monday is one of the seven days of the week.

money Money is the coins or bank notes you use when you buy something.

mongrel A mongrel is a dog which is a mixture of two or more kinds.

monkey A monkey is an animal that lives in hot countries. It has a long tail and strong hands.

month A month is a measure of time. There are 12 months in a year.

moon The moon is a planet. It goes round the earth once every four weeks.

moor A moor is an area of land with poor soil. It is covered mainly with grass and heather.

moose A moose is a large North American deer. It has very flat antlers.

mop A mop is a tool for washing dishes. It has a handle with cloth, sponge or pieces of string fixed to the end. Some mops are used for washing the floor. These have longer handles.

morning is the part of the day before noon.

mortar is a mixture of cement, sand and water. It is used in building, to hold bricks together.

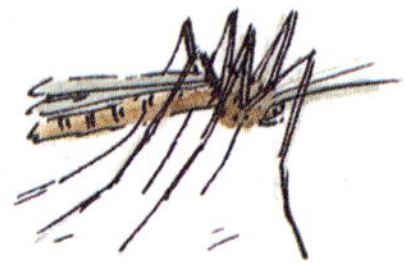

mosquito A mosquito is a small flying insect which lives in damp places. It bites people and animals.

moss is a very small green plant. It grows on damp ground, stone or wood.

moth A moth is an insect with wings.

motor A motor is part of a vehicle or machine. The motor uses fuel to make the vehicle or machine work.

motorway A motorway is a large road. Motorways are specially built for fast travel over long distances.

mountain A mountain is a raised part of the earth's surface. Mountains are very high, with steep sides. They are usually difficult to climb.

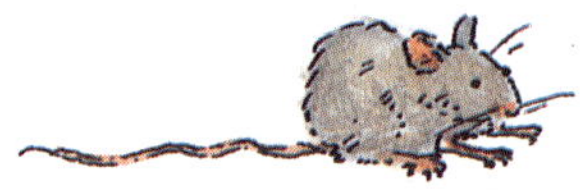

mouse A mouse is a small, furry animal with a long tail.

moustache (say merstosh) A man's moustache is the hair that grows on his upper lip.

mouth Your mouth is the opening that you put your food into when you eat. People, animals, fish and insects have mouths. Birds have beaks.

move
1 When someone or something moves they change their position. They do not stay still.
2 When you move an object you put it somewhere.

movement
1 When you make a movement you move part of your body.
2 If you see or hear a movement you notice someone or something moving.

mow If a person mows an area of grass, they cut it with a lawn mower.

mud is a wet and sticky mixture of earth and water. Mud becomes hard when it dries. In some countries it is used to build houses.

muddle If something such as papers are in a muddle, they are all mixed up.

mug A mug is a large deep cup. It usually has straight sides and a handle. Mugs do not usually have saucers.

mumps is an illness usually caught by children. If you get mumps your neck swells and your throat hurts.

murder To murder means to kill someone on purpose.

murmur
1 A murmur is a soft, low sound.
2 If you murmur you say something very quietly.

muscle (say mussel) Muscles are things in your body. They loosen and tighten to help you move.

museum A museum is a place or a building where you can see collections of important things. Some museums have works of art. Some have stuffed animals or birds. Many museums tell the story of something such as photography, vehicles, or fabrics. Most big towns have a museum.

mushroom A mushroom is a small plant. It has a short, thick stem with a round top. It looks like a tiny umbrella.

music is made up of sounds which are put together in a pattern. The sounds are usually made by a special instrument such as a piano or guitar. When music is made by a human voice it is called singing.

musket A musket is a gun with a long barrel. It fires lead balls instead of bullets. Muskets were used before rifles were invented.

mustard is a yellow or brown paste. It tastes hot and spicy. People often have a small amount of mustard with meat.

mystery
1 A mystery is something strange that cannot be explained.
2 A mystery story is one in which strange things happen. These things are usually explained at the end of the story.

nail
1 A nail is a small piece of metal with a point on one end. It usually has a flat top that you can hit with a hammer. Nails are sometimes used to join two pieces of wood together.
2 Your nails are the thin hard areas that cover the end of each of your fingers and toes.

name A name is what somebody or something is called.

narrow (narrower, narrowest) Something that is narrow is a very short distance from one side to the other.

nasty (nastier, nastiest)
1 Someone who is nasty is very unkind.
2 Something that is nasty is very unpleasant.

native
1 A native of a particular country is someone who was born there.
2 Your native country is the country where you were born.

natural is used to describe things that are not made by people. Trees, rocks and rivers are natural things.

nature is everything in the world that is not caused by human beings.

naughty (naughtier, naughtiest) A child who is naughty behaves badly.

navigate Someone who navigates a ship or aircraft works out which way to go.

navy
1 A navy is one of the forces that a country uses for fighting. Navies use ships to fight at sea.
2 Navy blue is a very dark blue colour.

near (nearer, nearest)
1 If you are near to something, you are only a short distance from it.
2 If something happens near to a paticular point in time, it happens close to it: *It happens somewhere near the beginning of the story.*

nearly means almost, but not quite: *I nearly caught him, but he ran away at the last moment.*

neat (neater, neatest) Something that is neat is very tidy and clean.

neck Your neck is the part of your body which joins your head to the rest of your body.

necklace A necklace is a piece of jewellery which is worn round the neck.

need
1 If you need something, you must have it in order to live and be healthy: *They need food and medicine.*
2 Sometimes you need something to help you do a particular job: *Now I need a paintbrush.*

needle
1 A needle is a small, very thin piece of metal used for sewing. It has a hole in one end and a sharp point at the other. You put thread through the hole.
2 A knitting needle is a thin stick that is used for knitting.
3 The thin leaves on pine trees are called needles.

negative
1 A negative is a piece of film from a camera. You can get your photographs printed from a negative.

neighbour A neighbour is someone who lives near you.

nervous
1 Someone who is nervous is easily frightened.
2 If you are nervous about something, you are slightly worried about it.

nest A nest is a home that an animal makes for its young.

net
1 Net is material made from threads. The threads are knotted or woven together, leaving holes in between. Net is sometimes called netting.
2 A net is a piece of netting which is stretched across a tennis court.
3 A net is also a bag made from netting. It is sometimes fixed to the end of a pole. It is used to catch animals, especially fish or butterflies.

never means no time in the past or future: *You must never cross the road without looking carefully.*

new (newer, newest)
1 Something that is new has just been made or built: *They have just built some new houses close to us.*
2 A new discovery is something that has not been noticed before: *Scientists have found a new star.*

news is information about things which have just happened: *I've got some good news. James has asked me to his party.*

newspaper A newspaper is sheets of paper which are printed and sold regularly. Daily newspapers are printed every day from Monday to Saturday. Others are sold once a week. Newspapers give information about things that have happened and are happening. They also have other interesting things such as puzzles and cartoons.

newt A newt is a small creature rather like a lizard. It has a moist skin, short legs and a long tail. Newts live partly on land and partly in water. Female newts lay eggs which hatch into tadpoles. The tadpoles gradually turn into tiny newts.

nib A nib is a small pointed piece of metal at the end of a pen. It holds ink as you write.

nibble
1 If you nibble something, you eat it slowly by taking small bites out of it.
2 If a small animal such as a mouse nibbles something, it takes small bites out of it quickly.

nice (nicer, nicest)
1 You say something is nice when you like it: *This cake is nice... Those flowers are nice.*
2 If you are nice to people, you are friendly and kind.
3 If the weather is nice, it is warm and pleasant.

nickname A nickname is a name that is given to a person by friends or family.

night The night is the time between evening and morning when it is dark outside.

nightingale A nightingale is a small brown European bird. The male has the most beautiful song of all birds. It sings after dark as well as during the day.

nimble (nimbler, nimblest) Someone who is nimble can move quickly and lightly.

noble (nobler, noblest)
1 Someone who is noble is honest, brave and unselfish.
2 A person of noble birth belongs to the family of someone such as a Duke or Baron.

nocturnal An animal that is nocturnal is active mostly at night.

noise A noise is a sound that someone or something makes.

nonsense is words that do not make sense.

non-stick A non-stick cooking pan is lined with a layer of special material. This stops food sticking to the pan.

noon is 12 o'clock in the middle of the day.

north is one of the four main compass points. If you face the point where the sun rises, north is on your left.

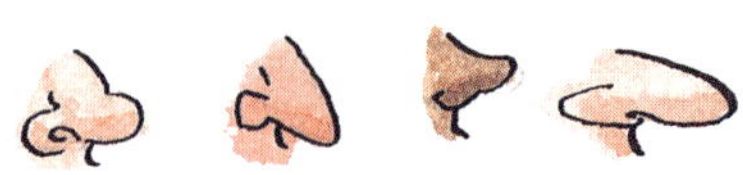

nose Your nose is the part of your face that sticks out above your mouth. It is used for smelling and breathing.

nostril Your nostrils are the two openings at the end of your nose. You breathe through your nostrils.

note

1 A note is a short letter.

2 A bank note is paper that is used as money.

3 A note is also a sound made by singing, or by playing a musical instrument.

notice

1 A notice is a sign which tells people something: *There was a notice which said 'Cameras are not allowed in the museum.'*

2 If you notice something, you pay attention to it: *They suddenly noticed it was getting late, and began to run.*

novel

1 A novel is a long written story. Novels are not true stories. They are made up by the writers.

2 Something that is novel is new and interesting.

now

1 Now means the present time.

2 Just now means a very short time ago.

November is the eleventh month of the year. It has 30 days.

nuisance

1 If you say that someone or something is a nuisance, you mean they annoy you.

2 If you make a nuisance of yourself, you behave in a way that irritates other people.

nun A nun is a woman who has made a special set of religious promises. Nuns live in large groups in a place called a convent. Some nuns live away from other people. Some nuns teach, or help to look after people.

nursery

1 A nursery is a room where the young children of a family play and sleep.

2 A nursery is also a place where very young children from different families can be looked after during the day.

3 A nursery can also be a place where plants are grown and sold.

nut

1 A nut is the hard fruit of certain trees, such as walnuts and chestnuts.

2 A nut is also a small piece of metal with a hole in it. It screws on to a bolt to fasten things together.

nylon is a strong, man-made material. It can be used for making fabrics for things such as curtains or clothes.

oak An oak is a large tree. It loses its leaves in the winter. The fruit of an oak tree is an acorn.

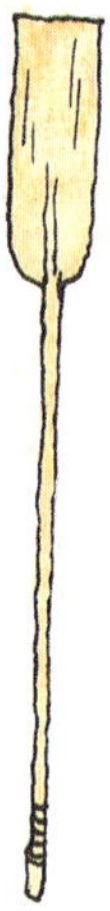

oȧr An oar is a long pole that is used for rowing a boat. It has a wide, flat piece on the end that goes in the water. The flat piece is called the blade.

oasis An oasis is a place in a desert where there is water, so that plants can grow.

obey If you obey someone, you do as they say.

object An object is a thing that you can touch and see, for example a toy or a book. Living things such as people and animals are not called objects.

ocean An ocean is one of the five very large seas on the Earth's surface.

October is the tenth month of the year. It has 31 days.

octopus An octopus is a sea creature. It has eight long arms called tentacles. It uses its tentacles to catch its food.

odd (odder, oddest)
1 If you say something is odd, you mean it is strange or unusual.
2 Odd things are those which do not belong in a pair or a set: *You can't go out like that – you're wearing odd socks.*

offer
1 If you offer something to someone, you ask them if they would like to have it: *She didn't bring anything to eat, so he offered her a bite of his apple.*
2 If you offer to do something, you say you will do it, without being asked: *Their neighbour was ill, so they offered to do his shopping.*

office An office is a room where someone works. Offices usually have lots of papers and books in them.

officer
1 An officer is an important person in an organization such as the armed forces.
2 Members of the police force are also called officers.

often If something happens often, it happens many times, or most of the time.

oil
1 Oil is a smooth, thick liquid that is used to keep machines running smoothly. It is also used for fuel.
2 Oil can also be made from plants or animals. These kinds of oil can sometimes be used for cooking.

ointment An ointment is a smooth, thick mixture that you put on sore skin to help it get better.

old (older, oldest)
1 Someone who is old has lived for many years.
2 Something that is old has been there for many years: *These walls are very old. They were built five hundred years ago.*

olive An olive is a small green or black oily fruit with a stone in the middle. Olives can be eaten, but they have a bitter taste. Olives can also be pressed to make olive oil.

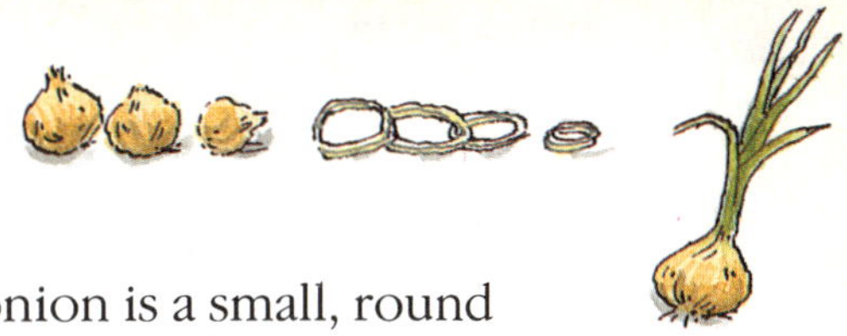

onion An onion is a small, round vegetable. It grows underground. It has a strong, sharp smell and taste. An onion is made up of thin white layers with a papery brown skin on the outside.

only
1 You say only when you mean one person or thing, and not the others: *He's only interested in football.*
2 Only also means one and no more: *He was the only boy in the group.*
3 An only child is someone who has no brothers or sisters.
4 You can say only when something is not very important: *I thought it was an unusual bird, but it was only a sparrow.*

open
1 If you open a door, you move it so that people can go through it.
2 If you open a box or a bottle you take the lid off, or unfasten it.
3 When a place such as a shop or a library is open, you can use it.
4 When flowers open, they change from being buds. Their petals spread out.

opening An opening is a hole or space that things or people can go through.

opera An opera is a musical play in which most of the words are sung.

opposite
1 If one person or thing is opposite another, they are on the other side of something: *In the train I sat opposite a small boy.*
2 The opposite of something is the thing that is most different from it: *Hot is the opposite to cold.*

orang-utan An orang-utan is a large ape with long arms. It comes from the rain forests of Borneo and Sumatra.

orbit An orbit is the curved path in space that is followed by one object going round a larger object; for example, a planet going round the sun.

orchard An orchard is an area of land where fruit trees are grown.

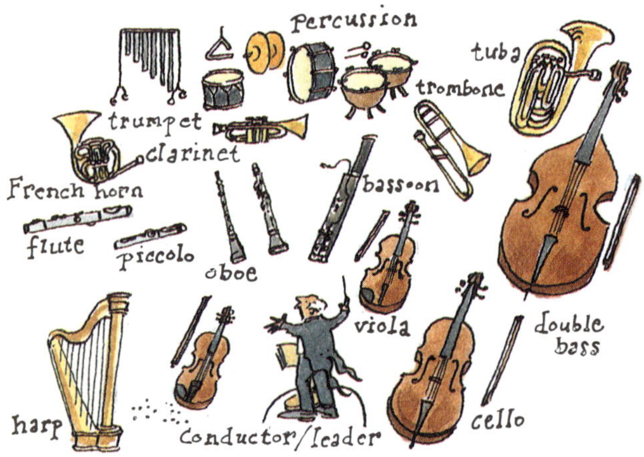

orchestra (say orkestra) An orchestra is a large group of musicians who play different instruments together.

order
1 Order is the way a set of things is organized. Names are often written in alphabetical order.
2 An order is something you are told to do.
3 If you are ordering something, for example in a restaurant, you ask for it to be brought to you.

ordinary Something that is ordinary is not special in any way.

ore is rock or earth with metal such as tin or iron in it.

organ
1 An organ is part of your body that does a special job. For example, your heart, lungs and stomach are organs.
2 An organ is also a large musical instrument. It has a lot of pipes of different lengths. It is played rather like a piano. As you press the keys, air is forced through the pipes to make different sounds.

organization (also spelled organisation) An organization is a large group of people who have particular aims. The police force and the Post Office are organizations.

organize (also spelled organise) If you organize something, you make all the arrangements for it so that everything happens as planned: *John, will you organize the picnic? Last time, we forgot the sandwiches.*

ornament An ornament is a small object that you have in your home because you think it is attractive and pleasant to look at.

ostrich An ostrich is the largest living bird. It cannot fly, but it can run very fast. Ostriches live in sandy places in Africa. Their eggs are very large, weighing more than a kilo each.

other
1 When you say other things or other people you can mean more of the same kind: *He found it hard to make friends with other children.*
2 You can also use other to mean different: *We got lost last time. I think we'll try some other way.*
3 If you say something happened the other day, you mean it happened not long ago.
4 Every other day means one day in every two, with a day in between: *We meet every other day, on Mondays, Wednesdays and Fridays.*

otherwise You say otherwise to explain what will happen if you don't do something: *I'd better take an umbrella, otherwise I'll get soaked.*

otter An otter is an animal with brown fur, short legs and a long tail. Otters live in and around lakes and rivers. They swim well with their webbed feet. They catch fish and small animals for food. Otters are very playful, even when they are adult.

outside
1 The outside of a building is the part that you can see when you walk round it without going in
2 Outside means in the open air: *Let's go outside. It's hot in here.*

oval An oval is a shape like an egg.

oven An oven is part of a cooker. It is like a metal box with a door. Food is put in an oven to be baked or roasted.

overboard If someone falls overboard, they fall over the side of a ship into the water.

overseas means belonging to countries that are on the other side of a sea or ocean.

overtake If you overtake someone, you pass them because you are moving faster than they are.

owe
1 If you owe money to someone, you need to pay it back because they have lent it to you.
2 If you owe someone something such as thanks, you feel grateful to them. Usually this is because they have been kind or helpful to you.

owl An owl is a bird with a flat face and large eyes. There are many kinds of owl. Usually owls hunt at night for small animals.

own
1 If you own something, it belongs to you.
2 If you are on your own, you are alone.
3 If you own up to something wrong, you say that you did it.

oxygen is a gas that forms part of the air we breathe. Oxygen is needed by most plants, animals and insects. Things will not burn without oxygen.

oyster An oyster is a flat shellfish. Some oysters can be eaten. Some make pearls.

pack
1 A pack is a bag holding your belongings.
2 A pack is also a set of playing cards.
3 A pack of wolves or other animals is a group that hunts together.
4 When you pack, you put your clothes in a case or bag.

package A package is a small parcel.

pad
A pad is a number of pieces of paper which are fixed together on one side. You write on the paper and then tear it off the pad.

paddle
1 A paddle is a pole with a flat part at one or both ends.
2 If you paddle in the sea, you stand at the edge of the water, with your feet just under the surface.

padlock A padlock is a special kind of lock. It is used for fastening two things together.

page A page is one side of a piece of paper in a book, newspaper or magazine.

pageant A pageant is a show. It is usually about history, with people dressed in colourful costumes.

pagoda A pagoda is a tall building which it used as a temple. Pagodas can be seen in China, Japan and South East Asia.

pain is an unpleasant feeling that you have in part of your body if you have been hurt, or are ill.

painful
1 If part of your body is painful, it hurts. This is because it is injured or because there is something wrong with it.
2 Something that is painful causes you to feel pain: *My shoes are painful.*

paint is a coloured liquid that you put on to a surface.

painting A painting is a picture that has been painted.

pair A pair is a set of two things that are to be used together: *I need a new pair of shoes.*

palace A palace is a very large, important house, especially one which is the home of a king, queen, or president.

palm
1 The palm of your hand is the inside surface of it. Your fingers and thumb are not part of your palm.
2 A palm is a tree which grows in hot countries. It has long pointed leaves that grow out of the top of a tall trunk. Palm tree trunks have no branches.

panda A giant panda is a large black and white animal the size of a bear. It lives in the bamboo forests of China.

panic is a feeling of fear which is so great that you cannot think what to do.

pant If you pant, you breathe quickly and loudly with your mouth open. You usually pant when you have been doing something like running, which uses a lot of energy.

panther is another name for leopard. Black leopards are often called panthers.

pantomime A pantomime is a funny musical play for children. The stories for pantomimes are taken from fairy tales.

pants Pants is another word for trousers or knickers.

paper
1 Paper is the material that you write on or wrap things with.
2 A newspaper is also called a paper.

parachute A parachute is a large piece of thin cloth shaped like an umbrella.

parade A parade is a lot of people marching in the road on a special day.

parallel Two lines or other things that are parallel are the same distance apart all the way along: *The road along the sea front runs parallel with the sea.*

parcel A parcel is one or more objects wrapped in paper. This is usually done so that it can be sent by post.

parchment is the yellowish-cream skin of a sheep or goat. People used to write on parchment.

park
1 A park is an area of land with grass and trees, usually in a town. People go there to relax or enjoy themselves.
2 When someone parks a vehicle, they put it where it will not get in the way. Then they often leave it for a short period.

parliament The parliament of a country is a group of people who meet to make the country's laws.

parrot A parrot is a tropical bird with a curved beak.

particular When you talk about a particular person or thing, you mean just that person or thing and not others of the same kind.

party A party is a group of people having fun together.

pass
1 A mountain pass is a narrow way between two mountains
2 If you pass someone or something you go past them without stopping.
3 If you pass something to someone, you hand it to them.
4 If you pass a test or examination you are successful.

passage A passage is a long narrow space with walls on both sides.

paste
1 Paste is a thick, wet mixture which can be used to stick paper.
2 Paste is also a smooth mixture of food. You usually spread paste on bread or toast.

pastry is a food made from flour, fat and water. It is mixed into a dough and rolled flat. Pastry is used for making pies.

pasture is land that is used for farm animals to graze on.

pat If you pat something, you hit it gently, usually with your open hand.

patch A patch is a piece of material that you use to cover a hole in something such as clothing.

path A path is a strip of ground that people walk on.

patient
1 A patient is someone who is being treated by a doctor.
2 If you are patient, you are able to wait calmly for something.

patrol When people such as the police patrol a particular area they go round it to make sure there is no trouble or danger.

pattern A pattern is the particular way that something is organized. This can be lines and shapes on a surface, such as patterns on fabric.

pavement A pavement is a path with a hard surface. In towns there are usually pavements on each side of a street so that people can walk in safety.

paw The paw of an animal such as a cat or dog is its foot. Paws have claws at the front and soft pads underneath.

pay When a person pays someone, they give them money in exchange for work or for things that have been bought.

pea Peas are round green seeds which are eaten as a vegetable. They grow inside a covering called a pod.

peace
1 Peace is a feeling of quiet and calm.
2 When a country has peace or is at peace, it is not fighting a war.

peach A peach is a round, juicy fruit with a large stone in the centre.

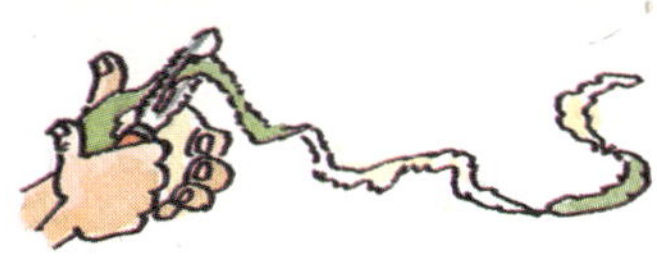

peacock A peacock is a large male bird of the pheasant family. The female is called a peahen.

peak
1 The peak of a mountain is the pointed top of it.
2 The peak of a cap is the part that sticks out at the front.
3 Peak times are periods which are very busy.

peanut Peanuts are small, hard seeds. They grow under the ground.

pear A pear is a sweet, juicy fruit which grows on trees.

pearl A pearl is a small, hard round object which grows inside the shell of an oyster.

pebble A pebble is a smooth, rounded stone which is found on seashores and river beds.

peck When a bird pecks it bites at something with a sudden forward movement of its beak.

peculiar If you say something is peculiar, you mean it is strange or unusual.

pedal The pedals on a cycle are the two parts that you push with your foot to make it move.

peel The peel of a fruit or vegetable is its skin.

peep If you peep at something you look at it very quickly.

peg
1 A peg on a wall or door is a thin piece of wood, metal or plastic that is used to hang things on.
2 A peg is also a small object that is used to hold washing on a line.

pelican A pelican is a large water bird. It has a long beak with a soft lower part like a pouch.

pen A pen is a long, thin tool with which you write in ink. There are different sorts of pen, such as ballpoint, felt tip or fountain pen.

pencil A pencil is an object that you use for writing or drawing. It is made from a long, thin piece of wood with graphite in the middle. The graphite makes a dark mark on paper.

pendulum A pendulum is a large weight which hangs from a clock. It swings from side to side to keep the clock going at the right speed.

penguin A penguin is a large black and white bird found in the Antarctic. Penguins cannot fly. They use their wings for swimming in the water.

penknife A penknife is a small knife with blades that fold into the handle.

pentagon A pentagon is a shape which has five straight sides.

people are men, women and children.

pepper Pepper is a hot-tasting powder which is used to flavour food.

perch
1 A perch is a fish that lives in lakes, ponds and rivers.
2 A perch is also a short piece of wood for a bird to stand on.

perfect
1 Something that is perfect is done so well that it could not be done better.
2 Perfect also means new or undamaged.

performance
1 A performance is doing something in front of people; for example, acting or dancing.
2 The performance of a vehicle is its ability to start quickly and to go fast.

perfume
1 A perfume is a pleasant smell: *The roses filled the air with perfume.*
2 Perfume is also a liquid that smells pleasant. Some people put it on their skins to make them smell nice.

period
1 A period is a particular length of time.
2 A period can also be a particular time in history; for example, the Victorian period.

periscope A periscope is a tube with mirrors in it.

permission If you are given permission to do something, someone has said you may do it.

person A person is a man, woman or child.

pet A pet is a tame animal that you keep and look after in your home.

petal The petals of a flower are the white or coloured main parts.

petrol is a liquid which is used as fuel in motor vehicles.

pheasant A pheasant is a long-tailed bird that is often hunted by human beings.

phone A phone is an instrument for talking to someone who is in another place. Phone is short for telephone.

photograph A photograph is a picture that is made using a camera and film. Photographs are called photos for short.

piano A piano is a large musical instrument. It has a row of black and white keys. When the keys are pressed down, little hammers hit wire strings inside the piano. Each string makes a different sound.

pick
1 If you pick something or someone you choose them: *We need to pick three more people for our team.*
2 When you pick things such as flowers or fruit, you gather them.
3 If you pick something up, you lift it up from where it is.

pickles are vegetables or fruit which have been kept in vinegar or salt water. They have a strong, sharp taste.

picnic A picnic is a meal that you take with you and eat out of doors. People often have a picnic on the beach or in a field.

picture
1 A picture is a drawing, painting or photograph of people, places or things.
2 Film and television cameras also take pictures, and show them on screens.

pie A pie is fruit, vegetables or meat baked in pastry.

piece
1 A piece is a bit or a part of something.
2 The pieces in a board game are the specially shaped objects that you move on the board when you play.

pier A pier is a long platform which sticks out over the sea at some seaside towns. Piers usually have some kind of entertainment on them.

pig A pig is a farm animal. Pigs are rather fat. They have short legs, large ears and tiny tails. They do not have much hair on their skin. Male pigs are called boars, and female pigs are sows. Their babies are called piglets.

pigeon A pigeon is a bird. It is usually grey in colour. It has a fat body and a small head. Pigeons make a soft cooing sound.

pike A pike is a large fish that lives in rivers and lakes.

pile
1 A pile is a lot of things heaped up together.
2 A pile is also a number of things such as books which have been put one on top of the other.

pill A pill is medicine that is made into a small round object that can be swallowed whole.

pillar A pillar is a tall post made of something such as stone or brick. It usually helps to hold up a building.

pillow A pillow is a bag filled with soft material to rest your head on in bed.

pin A pin is a very small thin piece of metal with a point at one end. Pins can be pushed through things such as paper or cloth to hold them together.

pinafore
1 A pinafore is a sort of apron that is worn to keep clothes clean.
2 A pinafore dress is a dress with no sleeves. It is usually worn over a blouse or sweater.

pinch
1 A pinch of something such as salt is the amount that you can hold between your thumb and first finger.
2 If someone pinches you, they squeeze part of you quickly between their thumb and first finger.

pine A pine is a tall evergreen tree. It has thin, sharp leaves called needles. The seeds of pine trees are held in cones on the branches of the tree.

pineapple A pineapple is a large, oval fruit. It is sweet and juicy. Pineapples grow in the tropics on plants which have stiff, fleshy leaves.

pipe
1 A pipe is a long hollow tube. It is usually made of metal or plastic. Pipes are used to carry liquids or gas.
2 A pipe is also an object which is used for smoking tobacco.

pistol A pistol is a small gun that can be fired from one hand.

pit
1 A pit is a large hole that has been dug in the ground.
2 A pit is also a coal mine.

pitch
1 A pitch is an area of ground where games such as hockey and football are played.
2 When you pitch a tent you put it up so that you can use it.

pity If you feel pity for someone, you feel sorry for them.

place
1 A place is somewhere such as a particular area or building: *Let's find a place to eat.*
2 When something takes place, it happens.

plaice A plaice is a sea fish with a flat body.

plait (say plat) If you plait a length of hair, you divide it into three lengths. Then you twist them together, putting them over and under until they make one thick length.

plan
1 A plan is a drawing that shows what something looks like from above.
2 If you say you have a plan, you mean you have thought of a way of doing something.
3 If you plan what you are going to do, you decide exactly how you are going to do it.

plane A plane is a flying vehicle. It has wings, and one or more engines.

planet A planet is a large, round object in space that goes round a star. Earth is one of the nine planets that go round the sun.

plank A plank is a long flat piece of wood.

plant
1 A plant is anything that grows in the soil.
2 When you plant something such as flowers or trees, you put them in the ground so that they will grow.

plastic is a man-made material. It is light in weight. It can be made into different shapes. It does not break easily. Plastic is used to make all sorts of things, such as buckets, bowls and plates.

Plasticine is a soft material like clay. It can be used to make models.

plate A plate is a flat dish that is used to hold food.

platform
1 A platform is a raised area in a hall. It is for people to stand on so that they can be seen more easily.
2 A platform is also the area in a railway station where you wait for the train.

play
1 A play is a story which is acted on the stage, or on radio or television.
2 When you play, you spend time doing enjoyable things.

pleasant (say plezant) (pleasanter, pleasantest)
1 You say someone is pleasant when they are friendly and easy to talk to.
2 Something that is pleasant is rather nice to look at or listen to.

please
1 You say please when you are asking someone to do something: *Could you reach that for me, please?*
2 You also say please when you want something that someone has offered you: *Would you like another piece of cake? – Yes, please.*
3 If you please someone, you make them feel happy.

pleasure is a feeling of happiness or enjoyment.

plenty If there is plenty of something, there is more than enough of it: *Help yourself to some apples. We've got plenty.*

plimsolls are shoes made of strong cotton material with a flat rubber sole.

plough A plough is a large farming tool with sharp blades. It is pulled by a tractor, or an animal such as a horse. As the plough moves over the ground it turns the soil ready for planting.

pluck When someone plucks a musical instrument such as a guitar they pull the strings with their fingers and then let them go.

plug
1 A plug is a thick piece of rubber or plastic that fits in the drain hole of a bath or washbasin.
2 A plug is also a small object that joins equipment to the electricity supply.

plum A plum is a small fruit with a thin dark red or yellow skin. It has a large stone in the middle.

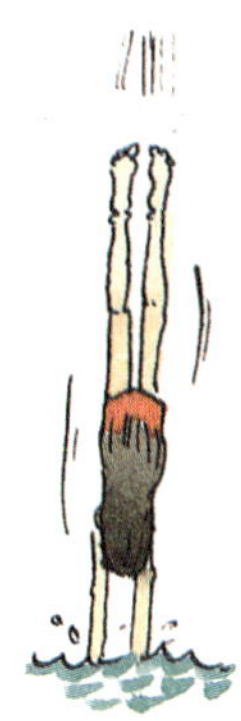

plunge If someone plunges into the water, they dive or throw themselves into it.

pocket A pocket is a small bag that is sewn into clothing. Pockets are used to carry small things such as handkerchiefs or coins.

pod A pod is a seed cover. Peas and beans grow inside pods.

poem A poem is a piece of writing. Poems often have short lines, which sometimes rhyme. The lines usually have a particular rhythm.

point
1 A point is a particular spot or place.
2 The point of something such as a pin is the sharp end of it.
3 In a game or sport, a point is part of the score.
4 If you point at something, you show it to somebody by using your finger.

poison is something that harms or kills people or animals if it is taken into their body.

polar bear A polar bear is a large white bear that lives near the North Pole.

police The police are an organization whose job is to protect people and their belongings. They also make sure people obey the law.

polish is something that you put on the surface of an object. It cleans and protects it, and makes it shine.

polite (politer, politest) Someone who is polite is well behaved and thinks about other people's feelings.

pollen is a fine powder found in flowers. It helps to make seeds grow.

polytechnic A polytechnic is a college where people can go after leaving school.

polythene is a thin plastic material. It is often made into bags.

pond A pond is a small lake.

pony A pony is a kind of horse. It is smaller than an ordinary horse.

pool A pool is a small area of still or slow-moving water.

poor (poorer, poorest)
1 Someone who is poor has very little money and few belongings.
2 If someone has poor eyesight they cannot see very well.

poppy A poppy is a plant with a large flower. Wild poppies are bright red.

popular
1 Someone who is popular is liked by most of the people in a particular group.
2 Something that is popular is liked by a lot of people.

pork is meat from a pig.

porpoise (say porpus) A porpoise is a sea animal. It looks like a dolphin or a small whale.

porridge is a thick, sticky food made from oats. The oats are cooked in water or milk. Porridge is eaten hot, usually for breakfast.

port
1 A port is a town which has a harbour.
2 The port side of a ship or aircraft is the left side when you are facing towards the front.

porthole A porthole is a small round window in the side of a ship.

position
1 The position of someone or something is the place where they are at a particular moment.
2 Someone's position can also be the way they are sitting or standing: *Try and stay in that position while I draw you.*

post
1 Post is letters or parcels delivered by the post office.
2 A post is a strong piece of wood or metal fixed upright in the ground.
3 If you post a letter you send it to someone by putting it in a post-box.

postcode A postcode is the letters and numbers at the end of an address.

poster A poster is a large notice that is put on a wall or notice board. It tells people about something. Posters often have pictures on them.

potato A potato is a round vegetable that grows under the ground. Potatoes can be boiled, baked or fried. They can also be made into chips or crisps.

pottery is articles such as dishes and ornaments that are made from clay.

pouch

1 A pouch is a small bag for keeping things in.
2 A pouch can also be a pocket of skin on an animal. Female kangaroos and other marsupials have a pouch on their stomach. Their babies grow in this pouch. Hamsters have pouches in their cheeks, for storing food.

pound
1 A pound is a unit of money used in Britain. One pound is divided up into 100 pence.
2 A pound is also a measure of weight. One pound is nearly half a kilogram.
3 If you pound something, you keep hitting it hard.

pour If you pour a liquid you tip it out of a container.

powder is something which has been ground into very tiny pieces.

power
1 If someone has power, they have control over other people.
2 The power of something such as the wind or the sea is the strength that it has.
3 Power is energy that can be used to make things work. For example, cars need power to make them go along the road. They get their power from fuel such as petrol.

pram A pram is a small carriage for babies.

prawn A prawn is a small shellfish. It is like a large shrimp.

pray If you pray, you speak to the God that you believe in, to give thanks or to ask for help.

prayer A prayer is all the words you say when you are praying.

precious
1 Something that is precious is worth a lot of money.
2 You also say something is precious if it is very important to you.

precipice A precipice is a very steep side on a mountain or rock.

prehistoric Something that is prehistoric belongs to the time before history was written down.

present
1 A present is something nice you give to someone, for example on their birthday.
2 The present is the period of time that is taking place now.
3 If someone is present somewhere, they are there: *Both her parents were present when she was given the prize.*

preserve
1 If you preserve something, you do something to keep it the way it is.
2 To preserve food means to stop it from going bad. There are several ways of preserving food. It can be frozen, dried, pickled, tinned or bottled.

president
1 The president of an organization is the head of it.
2 The president of a country is the head of the country.

press
1 If you press something against something else you hold it there firmly: *She pressed the phone against her ear.*
2 If someone presses clothes, they iron them to smooth the creases.

pretend If you pretend to be someone, or pretend to be doing something, you act as though it were real, although it is not: *Let's pretend to be doctors and nurses.*

pretty (prettier, prettiest) Someone who is pretty is nice to look at.

prevent If you prevent someone from doing something, you stop them doing it.

prey The prey of an animal is the creatures that it hunts for food.

price The price of something is the amount of money that you must pay in order to buy it.

prick If something sharp such as a pin pricks you, it makes a tiny hole in your skin.

primrose A primrose is a small wild plant. It has pale yellow flowers in spring.

prince A prince is the son of a king or queen.

princess A princess is the daughter of a king or queen.

print
1 A print is one of the photographs from a film.
2 A print is also a footprint or a fingerprint.
3 When someone prints something such as a poster or a newspaper, they use a machine to make lots of copies of it.
4 If you print words, you write in letters that are not joined together.

prison A prison is a building where people are kept when they have done something very bad.

private
1 If something is private, it is for one person or group only: *All the rooms have a private bath.*
2 Private talks are those that are held between a few people. The things that are said are kept secret from everyone else.

prize A prize is something that is given to someone as a reward.

probably You say probably when you think something might be true, but you are not sure: *We shall probably be home before 4 o'clock.*

procession A procession is a line of people walking or riding through the streets for a special reason.

programme
1 A programme is a plan of things that will take place.
2 A radio or television programme is the thing such as a play or talk that is being broadcast.

project A project is a study of something: *We are doing a project on trees at school.*

promise If you promise that you will do something, you mean you really will do it.

prong The prongs of a fork are the long pointed parts. A fork usually has three or four prongs.

propeller A propeller is the blades that turn to drive an aeroplane or ship.

proper
1 Proper means right: *Put those things back in the proper place.*
2 You can also use proper to mean real: *You need a proper screwdriver for that job.*

protect To protect someone or something means to keep them safe from harm or damage.

proverb A proverb is a short sentence that people often say. Proverbs give advice about life. For example, the proverb 'Look before you leap' means that you should think carefully before you do something.

provide If you provide something for someone you give it to them so that they have it when they need it.

prune
1 A prune is a dark purple plum that has been dried.

2 When someone prunes a tree, they cut off some of the branches so that it will grow better.

public Something which is public can be used by anyone.

pudding A pudding is a cooked sweet food. It is usually eaten after the main part of a meal.

puddle A puddle is a small pool of liquid on the ground or floor. You can see puddles of water on the ground when it has been raining.

pull
1 When you pull something, you hold it firmly and move it towards you.
2 When an animal or vehicle pulls something such as a cart or trailer, it is fixed to them so that it moves along behind them.

pump A pump is a machine which is used to force gas or liquid to move the way it is wanted.

pumpkin A pumpkin is a very large, orange-coloured fruit with a thick skin. It is soft inside with a lot of pips. Pumpkins grow on plants which trail across the ground.

puncture A puncture is a small hole in a tyre. When a tyre has a puncture, the air inside escapes and the tyre goes flat.

pupil
1 The pupils of a school are the children who go there to learn.
2 The pupil in your eye is the small round black hole in the centre. The size of your pupils changes with the light. When it is bright, your pupils are very small. When the light is low, your pupils grow larger.

puppet A puppet is a kind of doll that you can move. Some puppets have strings fixed to them which you can pull. Others are made so that you can put your hand inside.

puppy A puppy is a young dog.

purpose
1 If something is made for a purpose, it is made to be used in that way: *I use this as a hammer, but it wasn't made for that purpose.*
2 If you do something on purpose you mean to do it. It does not happen by accident.

push When you push something you press it hard.

puzzle
1 A puzzle is something that is hard to understand.
2 A puzzle can also be a game or toy that you have to think about carefully; for example, a crossword puzzle.

pyjamas A pair of pyjamas is a loose jacket and trousers that a person can wear in bed.

pyramid
1 A pyramid is a solid shape with a flat base. It has flat sides the shape of triangles. The sides slope upwards and inwards to a point.
2 A pyramid is also an ancient building made of stone, in the shape of a pyramid. There are pyramids in Egypt, and in Mexico.

quantity A quantity is an amount that you can measure or count: *We shall need a large quantity of food for the weekend.*

quarrel If people quarrel, they have an angry argument.

quarry
1 A quarry is an animal that is being hunted.
2 A quarry is also a deep hole that has been dug in a piece of land. Quarries are dug to provide materials such as stone for building and other work.

quarter
1 A quarter is one of four equal parts of something.
2 When you are telling the time, quarter to a particular hour means 15 minutes before or after that hour: *It's either quarter to three, or it's quarter past three.*

queen
1 A queen is a woman who rules a country. Queens are not chosen by the people. They are born into a royal family.
2 The wife of a king is also called a queen.
3 In the insect world, a queen is a large female bee, ant or wasp which can lay eggs. There is usually only one queen in each group of insects.

question A question is words you say or write when you want to ask something.

queue A queue is a line of people waiting for their turn. People sometimes queue in shops or at bus stops. A line of vehicles can also be called a queue, if they are waiting to move.

quick (quicker, quickest)
1 Someone or something that is quick moves with great speed.
2 Something that is quick lasts only a short time: *I'll have a quick look at it later.*
3 Someone who is quick is bright, and able to understand things with great speed.

quickly If you do something quickly, you do it as fast as you can.

quiet (quieter, quietest)
1 Someone or something that is quiet makes only a small amount of noise.
2 If a place is quiet, there is very little noise there.
3 If someone tells you to be quiet, they do not want you to say anything at all.
4 A quiet person always behaves in a calm and gentle way.

quietly If you do or say something quietly, you make very little noise.

quilt A quilt is a cover filled with feathers or some other light, warm material. People often have a quilt over them in bed.

quite
1 Quite means rather: *I think he's quite nice.*
2 Quite can also mean completely: *The work is now quite finished.*

quiz A quiz is a game or test. Someone tries to find out how much you know by asking you questions.

rabbit A rabbit is a small, furry animal with long ears. Rabbits are often kept as pets. Wild rabbits live in holes in the ground called burrows. A group of burrows is called a warren.

race
1 A race is a competition to see who is the fastest; for example, in running or swimming.
2 A race is also a large group of people who look alike in some way. Different races have for example different skin colour, or differently shaped eyes.

rack A rack is a frame that is used for holding things or for hanging things on. Racks are usually made with something such as hooks, pegs or bars.

radar is a way of showing the position and speed of ships and aircraft when they cannot be seen. Radio signals give the information on a screen.

radiator
1 A radiator is a hollow metal object that can be filled with liquid in order to heat a room. Radiators are usually connected by pipes to a boiler.
2 In a car, the radiator holds the water that is used to cool the engine.

radio A radio is a piece of equipment which receives sounds through the air. You can use a radio to listen to programmes that are broadcast.

raft A raft is a floating platform. Rafts are often made of large pieces of wood fixed together.

rag
1 A rag is a piece of old cloth that you can use to clean or wipe things.
2 Rags are old, torn clothes.

rage Someone who is in a rage is very, very angry.

ragged (say raggid)
1 Clothes that are ragged are old and torn, and rather dirty.
2 An edge that is ragged is uneven and rough.

raid A raid is a sudden attack against an enemy.

rail
1 A rail is a horizontal bar that is firmly fixed to posts. Rails are used as fences, or for people to lean on.
2 Rails are the heavy metal bars that trains run on.

railing A railing is a kind of fence made from metal bars.

railway A railway is a way of travelling and carrying things from one place to another. A locomotive pulls carriages or trucks along rails which are fixed to the ground.

rain is water that falls from the clouds in small drops.

rainbow A rainbow is an arch of different colours that can sometimes be seen in the sky.

raincoat A raincoat is a waterproof coat you wear when it is raining.

raise
1 If you raise something, you move it so that it is higher.
2 If you raise your voice, you speak more loudly.
3 Someone who raises children looks after them until they are grown up.

rake A rake is a garden tool.

ram If one vehicle rams another, it crashes into it with great force. This usually causes a lot of damage.

ranch In the United States, a ranch is a large farm for raising cattle, sheep or horses.

range A range is a row of hills or mountains.

rapid Something that is rapid is very quick.

rapids are parts of a river where the water moves very fast, often over rocks.

raspberry A raspberry is a small red fruit. It is soft and juicy, with a lot of small seeds called pips. Raspberries grow on bushes.

rat A rat is a small animal with a long scaly tail. It looks rather like a large mouse. Rats have very sharp teeth.

rattle
1 A rattle is a baby's toy that makes a noise when it is shaken.
2 When something rattles, it makes short, rapid knocking sounds: *Can you stop that window rattling?*

rattlesnake A rattlesnake is a poisonous American snake. It has bony rings at the end of its tail. These make a rattling sound when the snake shakes its tail.

raven A raven is a large bird. It belongs to the crow family. Ravens have shiny black feathers and a harsh call.

raw Food that is raw is not cooked.

ray A ray is a line of light.

razor A razor is a tool that people use to remove hair.

reach
1 When you reach a place you arrive there.
2 If you reach somewhere, you stretch out your hand: *I reached across the table for the salt.*

read
1 When you read, you look at words or symbols and understand what they mean.
2 When you read aloud, you say the words that are written.

real
1 Something that is real is true. It is not imaginary: *I've seen a real princess.*
2 You also say real when you mean the thing itself, and not a copy: *I've got a lovely pony made of velvet. But Jenny's got a real pony.*

reason The reason for something is why it happens: *I'm sorry I'm late. There is a good reason.*

receive When you receive something, you get it after it has been given or sent to you.

recipe A recipe tells you how to make something to eat or drink. It gives you a list of the things you need, and tells you how to mix and cook them.

recite When you recite something such as a poem, you say it aloud from memory.

record
1 A record is a round, flat piece of plastic. When it is played you can hear sounds such as music.
2 A record is also the very best performance of something: *In that race, he set a new record.*

rectangle A rectangle is a shape with four straight sides and square corners. It has two equal long sides and two equal short sides.

reed A reed is a plant with a tall, hollow stem. Reeds grow in large groups in or near water.

reef A reef is a long line of rocks or sand that is just below the surface of the sea.

reel A reel is an object shaped like a cylinder. It is used to hold long thin material such as thread or wire.

referee A referee is a person whose job is to control a sports match. Referees make sure that players follow the rules properly.

reflect
1 When a surface reflects rays of light or heat, the rays bounce back from the surface.
2 When a mirror reflects a person or thing it shows what they look like.

refuse If you refuse to do something you will not do it.

register
1 A register is a list of names or things that have happened.
2 When you register, you put your name on a list.

reign (say rain) The reign of a king or queen is the period during which they rule.

rein A rein is one of the leather straps that are used to control a horse.

reindeer A reindeer is a large deer that lives in cold northern parts of the world.

relax When you relax you stop worrying and feel more calm.

remain
1 If you remain in a place you stay there and do not go away.
2 The remains of something are the parts of it that are left when everything else has gone. For example, a fossil is the hardened remains of a prehistoric animal or plant.

remember If you can remember something, you can bring it back into your mind.

remove
1 If you remove something from somewhere, you take it away.
2 When you remove your clothing you take it off.

rent is the money that a person pays so that they will be allowed to use something that belongs to someone else. People often pay rent so that they can live in a house that is owned by somebody else.

repair If you repair something that has been damaged or is not working properly, you mend it.

repeat If you repeat something, you say it or do it again.

reply When you reply, you answer somebody.

report A report is something that is said or written about something that has happened.

reptile A reptile is a cold-blooded animal with a scaly skin. Female reptiles lay eggs. Tortoises, snakes and crocodiles are all reptiles.

rescue If a person rescues someone, they help them get away from danger.

reservoir A reservoir is a lake that is used for storing drinking water for a city or other area.

rest
1 The rest is all the things in a group that are left: *I've done some of the washing up. I'll do the rest tomorrow.*
2 When you rest you sit or lie down. You do not do anything active for a while.

restaurant A restaurant is a place where meals are served.

retreat When an army retreats, it moves away from the enemy.

return
1 When you return to a place, you go back there after you have been away.
2 If you return something to someone you give it back to them: *I must return that book to the library today.*

revolver A revolver is a hand gun. It can fire several bullets before it needs reloading.

reward A reward is something you are given for doing well.

rhinoceros A rhinoceros is a big animal. It has a very thick skin and one or two horns on its nose. Rhinoceroses live in Africa and Asia. They live on plants, especially grass. They are often called rhinos for short.

rhyme If two words rhyme, they have a similar sound. People often use words that rhyme at the ends of lines in poems: *I need a word to rhyme with dog. – How about fog?*

rhythm is a regular pattern of sound or movement. Music and dancing have rhythm.

rib Your ribs are the curved bones that go from your backbone to your chest. People and animals have 12 ribs on either side of their bodies. They protect the heart and other organs.

ribbon A ribbon is a long narrow piece of fine cloth. It is used for tying things together, or as a decoration.

rice is white grains which are boiled and eaten. In many countries rice is the main food.

rich (richer, richest) Someone who is rich has a lot of money or valuable things.

riddle A riddle is a kind of puzzle. You ask a question which has a funny answer.

ride
1 When a person rides a horse or bicycle, they sit on it and control its movements.
2 When you ride in a vehicle such as a car, you travel in it.

right Someone's right hand is the hand that most people write with.

rim
1 The rim of a container such as a cup is the edge that goes all the way round the top.
2 The rim of a circular object such as a wheel is the outside edge of it.

ring
1 A ring is an ornament people wear on a finger.
2 A ring can also be anything in the shape of a circle.
3 A ring is also the sound made by a bell.
4 If you ring someone, you call them on the telephone.

rip If someone rips something, they tear it violently with their hands or a knife: *She ripped open the envelope to see who the letter was from.*

ripe When fruit or grain is ripe, it is ready to be harvested or eaten.

ripple A ripple is a little wave on the surface of water.

rise
1 If something rises, it moves upwards.
2 When the sun or the moon rises, it appears above the horizon.

risk
1 A risk is a danger that something bad might happen.
2 If someone takes a risk, they do something knowing that it could be dangerous.

river A river is a large amount of fresh water flowing in a long curving line across the land. Rivers flow into the sea, a lake, or into another river.

road A road is a long, smooth, hard piece of ground. Roads are made so that vehicles can travel from place to place.

roar A roar is a very loud noise. For example, the noise made by wild animals such as lions is called a roar. You can also describe the noise made by traffic as a roar.

roast When someone roasts food such as meat, they cook it in an oven or over an open fire.

robin A robin is a small brown bird with a red neck and breast.

robot A robot is a machine which is programmed to do a number of things. Robots are often used in factories.

rock
1 Rock is the very hard material that is in the earth. Cliffs and mountains are made of rock.
2 Rock is also a kind of music.
3 There is a kind of sweet made in long sticks which is called rock.
3 When something rocks, it moves slowly backwards and forwards, or from side to side.

rocket A rocket is a missile that drives itself through the air.

rocky A place that is rocky is covered with rocks.

rod A rod is a long thin straight bar of something such as wood or metal.

rodent A rodent is a small mammal with sharp front teeth. Rats, mice, rabbits and squirrels are all rodents.

roll
1 A roll of something such as paper or tape is a long piece of it, wrapped round several times.
2 A roll is a very small loaf of bread for one person.
3 A roll is also a list of people's names.
4 When a round object such as a ball rolls, it moves along turning over and over.

roller
1 A roller is a large heavy wheel. Some rollers have handles on, and can be used in the garden, Larger rollers are fixed to vehicles. They are used to make roads flat.
2 Rollers are hollow tubes used for curling hair.

roof A roof is the covering on top of a building or vehicle.

rook A rook is a large black bird of the crow family. It has a harsh, loud cry.

room
1 A room is one of the parts of a house or other building. A room has its own walls and door. Halls and landings are not called rooms.
2 Room is space to move about in and to put things in: *We can't have the party here. There wouldn't be enough room for everybody.*

root
1 A root is the part of a plant that grows underground.
2 The root of a hair, tooth or nail is the part that you cannot see because it is covered with skin.

rope A rope is a piece of very thick, strong string.

rose A rose is a flower. There are many different kinds of rose. Most of them grow on very thorny stems. Some roses have a very pleasant smell.

rot
1 When vegetables and other foods rot, they go bad.
2 When something such as wood rots, it goes soft and can be easily pulled to pieces.

rough (rougher, roughest)
1 If something is rough, the surface is uneven and not smooth.
2 If the sea is rough, there are big waves.

round Something that is round is shaped like a ball, or a circle.

roundabout
1 A roundabout is a large machine at a fair. It has large toy animals or cars on it. Children can sit on the toys and go round and round.
2 A roundabout is also an island in the middle of the road at a place where several roads meet.

row (as in toe)
1 A row is a number of people or things arranged in a line.
2 When someone rows a boat, they make it move through the water by using oars.

royal
1 Someone who is royal belongs to the family of a king or queen.
2 Something that is royal is connected with a royal family.

rub When you rub something, you wipe it hard. You can rub with your hand alone, or you can use a cloth.

rubber
1 Rubber is a strong, stretchy material that is made from the sap of a tropical tree.
2 A rubber is a small piece of rubber that you use to get rid of pencil marks on paper.

rubbish
1 Rubbish is unwanted things.
2 Rubbish is also waste material such as used paper or empty tins.
3 If someone says that something is rubbish, they mean they think it is of very poor quality: *There is so much rubbish on television.*

rude (ruder, rudest) If someone is rude, they behave badly and are not polite: *It's rude to stare at people.*

rugby is a game played with an oval ball. Two teams try to score points by carrying the ball across a line, or by kicking the ball over a bar.

rule
1 Rules are directions that tell you what you are allowed to do and what you are not allowed to do. Rules are used in games, and in certain places such as schools.
2 To rule a country means to be in charge of the way a country works.
3 If you rule lines, you draw them using something that has a straight edge.

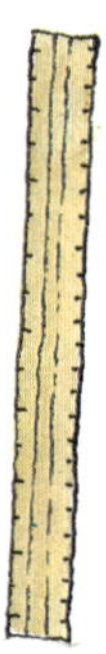

ruler
1 A ruler is a person such as a king, queen, or prime minister, who is the leader of a country.
2 A ruler is also a long flat piece of something such as wood or plastic, with straight edges.

run
1 When you run, you move on your feet faster than when you walk.
2 When a vehicle such as a train or bus runs somewhere, it travels at set times: *The bus runs every 20 minutes.*
3 If you run water, you make it flow from something such as a tap.

rung A rung is a wooden or metal bar that forms a step on a ladder.

runway A runway is a long, narrow strip of ground with a hard, level surface. Runways are used by aeroplanes when they are taking off or landing.

rush
1 A rush of air or water is the sound or feeling of it moving quickly.
2 Rushes are plants that grow near water.
3 If you rush somewhere, you go there quickly.

rust is a reddish-brown coating that forms on metal such as iron and steel if it is left in a damp place. Rust gradually destroys metal.

rustle A rustle is a soft sound made by something such as paper or leaves moving gently together.

rut A rut is a deep, narrow mark made in the ground by the wheels of vehicles.

rye is a cereal grown in cold countries. The grain from rye can be ground into flour to make bread.

sack A sack is a large, strong bag made of cloth or plastic. Sacks are used to carry or store things such as potatoes or coal.

sad (sadder, saddest) If you are sad, you are unhappy because something has happened that you do not like.

saddle A saddle is a seat for a rider on a horse or bicycle.

safari A safari is a journey to hunt or see wild animals.

safari park A safari park is a large fenced area of land where wild animals live and move around freely.

safe (safer, safest)
1 A safe is a strong metal cupboard with special locks. People keep money or valuable things in a safe.
2 If you are safe, you are not in any danger.
3 If something is safe it cannot cause harm: *Is this soap powder safe for wool?*
4 If something is in a safe place it cannot be lost or stolen.

sail
1 A sail is a large piece of material fixed to the mast of a ship or boat. The wind blows against the sail and pushes the ship or boat along.
2 A sail is also one of the flat pieces of wood on the top of a windmill. The wind drives the sails of a windmill.
3 To sail a boat means to make it move across water using its sails.

salmon (say sammon) A salmon is a large silvery fish which is good to eat. Salmon live in the sea, but they swim up rivers to lay their eggs.

salt is a white powder or crystal with a bitter taste. Salt is found in the earth and in sea water. It is used to flavour or preserve food.

same If two things are the same, they are exactly like each other in some way: *Look! Your dress is the same as mine.*

sand is very small grains of rock, shells and other material. Most deserts and beaches are made of sand.

sandal Sandals are light shoes for warm weather. The soles are held on by straps which go over your foot.

sandwich A sandwich is two slices of bread with a layer of food between them; for example, meat, cucumber or jam.

sap is the liquid that carries food through plants and trees.

sardine A sardine is a small seafish of the herring family which is eaten as food. Sardines are often preserved and sold in tins.

satchel A satchel is a bag, usually with a shoulder strap. School children often use satchels for carrying books.

satellite
1 A satellite is a natural object in space that moves around a larger object. For example, the moon is a satellite of the earth.
2 A satellite is also an object that is sent into space. It travels round the earth or another planet.

Saturday is one of the seven days of the week. It is the day after Friday and before Sunday.

sauce A sauce is a thick liquid, often made from vegetables or fruit. It is served with other food to add to the taste.

saucepan A saucepan is a deep metal cooking pot. It usually has a long handle. Most saucepans have lids.

saucer A saucer is a small curved plate to put a cup on.

sausage A sausage is a finely minced meat mixture put into a skin.

save
1 If you save someone or something, you help them to escape from harm or danger: *He fell in the river and his father dived in to save him.*
2 If you save money, you gradually collect it by not spending it as soon as you get it.

saw A saw is a tool for cutting wood and other materials. It has a blade with sharp teeth along one edge.

say When you say something, you speak words.

scald If you scald yourself you burn yourself with very hot liquid or steam.

scale
1 A scale is a series of musical notes that are played or sung in order.
2 A scale is also one of the small flat pieces of skin that cover the body of fish, snakes and other reptiles.

scales are a machine used to weigh people or things.

scar A scar is a mark that is left on the skin after a wound has healed.

scare Someone or something that scares you makes you feel frightened.

scarf A scarf is a piece of cloth that you wear round your neck to keep you warm. Scarves are often long and narrow.

scatter If you scatter things you throw or drop a lot of them all over an area.

scene (say seen) The scene of something is the place where it happened: *The police went to the scene of the crime.*

scent (say sent)
1 A scent is a pleasant smell.
2 Scent is a liquid that some people put on their skin to make them smell nice.
3 The scent of an animal is a smell that it leaves. Other animals can follow the scent when they are hunting it.

school is a place for teaching and learning.

science (say sy-ence) Science is the study of natural things. We learn about these things by looking and testing very carefully.

scientist (say sy-entist) A scientist is a person who finds out why things happen by doing tests and by careful study.

scissors (say sizzors) A pair of scissors is a small tool that is used for cutting paper and cloth. It has two sharp blades, and two rings for your thumb and fingers.

scooter
1 A scooter is a small, light motorcycle.
2 A scooter is also a child's toy. It has two wheels with a flat piece in between, and handlebars. You put one foot on the flat piece, and push yourself along with your other foot.

score The score in a game is the total number of points made by the two teams or players.

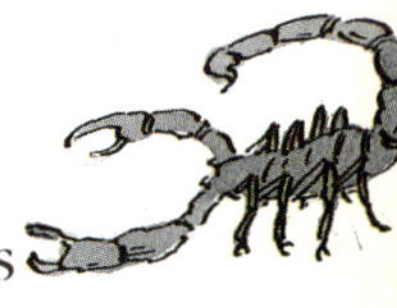

scorpion A scorpion is a small tropical animal of the spider family. It has a long curving tail with a poisonous sting on the end.

scramble If you scramble over rough or difficult ground, you move over it quickly, using your hands to help you.

scrap A scrap of something such as cloth or paper is a small piece of it.

scrape If you scrape something you take off its surface by dragging a knife across it.

scratch
1 A scratch is a small cut on your body.
2 If you scratch something, you damage it by making small cuts on it: *I fell into the hedge and scratched my bike.*
3 If you scratch part of your body, you rub your fingernails against your skin.

scream When someone screams they make a very loud, high cry. People usually scream if they are very frightened, or are in a lot of pain.

screen A screen is a flat, vertical surface on which a picture is shown. Television sets have screens.

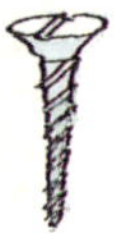

screw
1 A screw is a small sharp piece of metal, rather like a nail. It has a groove going round it, and a slot in the head. Screws are used to fix pieces of wood together.
2 If you screw something up, you twist it or squeeze it so that it gets very creased: *She screwed up the paper and threw it in the bin.*

scribble If you scribble words, you write them quickly and roughly.

scrub If you scrub something, you rub it clean, usually with a stiff brush and water.

sculpture A sculpture is an object that has been made by an artist. Sculptures are often made by carving stone or by modelling clay.

sea The sea is the salty water that covers about three quarters of the earth's surface.

seagull A seagull is a large bird that lives near the sea.

seal
1 A seal is a large animal that lives partly on land and partly in the sea.
2 If you seal an envelope you stick it down so that people cannot see what is inside.

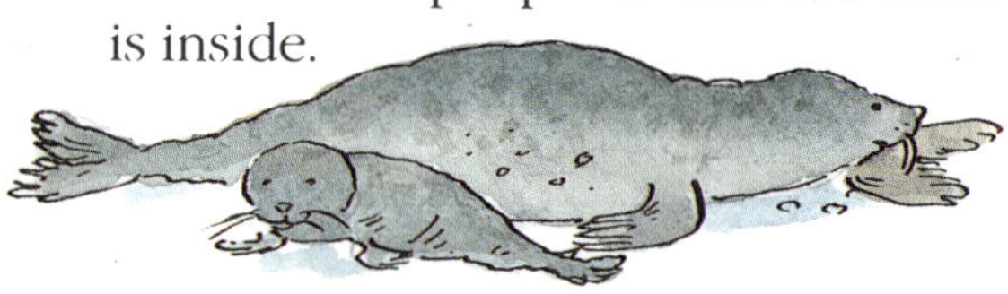

search If you search for something, you try to find it by looking very carefully.

season A season is one of the main periods of a year. Most parts of the world have four seasons: spring, summer, autumn and winter.

seat A seat is a place where you can sit; for example, a chair or stool.

seaweed is a plant that grows in the sea. There are many kinds of seaweed.

second
1 A second is a very short period of time. There are 60 seconds in one minute.
2 Something that is second in a series comes directly after the first: *I came second in that race.*

secret A secret is something that is known about by only a small number of people.

see When you see, you use your eyes to look at something.

seed A seed is the small hard part of a plant from which a new plant grows.

seem
1 If you say that someone seems, for example, to be happy or sad, you mean that is the way they look: *Tim seems to be a bit upset today.*
2 If you say something seems a certain way, you mean that is the way it feels to you: *I only had to wait for ten minutes, but it seemed like hours.*

seesaw A seesaw is a long board which is balanced on a fixed part in the middle. If you sit on one end, the other end goes up in the air.

selfish People who are selfish only think about themselves. They do not care about other people.

sell When someone sells something, they give it in exchange for money.

send
1 When you send something to someone, you arrange for it to be delivered to them. People often send things through the post.
2 If someone sends somebody somewhere, they tell them to go there: *She was sent home from school because she didn't feel well.*

senior
1 The senior people in an organization are the people who have the highest and most important jobs in it.
2 At a school or college, the seniors are the older pupils or students.

sense
1 Your senses are the powers you have to find out about the things around you. Most people have five senses. They are the senses of sight, smell, hearing, touch and taste.
2 Sense is the ability to know the right thing to do: *Why did you do that? You should have had more sense.*
3 If something makes sense, you can understand it.

sensible People who are sensible are good at deciding what to do. They do not do anything silly.

sentence A sentence is a group of words that mean something. If a sentence is written down, it begins with a capital letter and ends with a full stop.

separate If one thing is separate from another, the two things are apart from each other. They are not joined together.

September is the ninth month of the year. It has 30 days.

series
1 a series of things is a number of things of the same kind that follow each other.
2 A radio or television series is a set of programmes about the same thing.

serious
1 Things that are serious are important. They must be thought about carefully.
2 When people are serious, they mean what they say. They are not joking.
3 Serious people are usually quiet and do not laugh very much.

serve
1 If someone serves something such as a company or a country, they work for it.
2 If someone serves food and drink they give it to people, for example in a restaurant or at a meal.
3 If someone serves people in a shop they help them to buy what they want.

set
1 A set is a number of things of the same kind that belong together.
2 A set is also a television or radio.

settee A settee is a long seat for two or more people.

several means a small number of things or people. If you say several, you mean more than two or three, but not very many.

sew (say so) When someone sews they join pieces of cloth together by using a needle and thread.

sex The two sexes are the two groups that people and other living things are divided into. One sex is male and the other sex is female. Only animals of the female sex are able to have babies.

shade
1 Shade is the darkness that is caused when something stops sunlight reaching a place: *It was hot in the garden, so she sat in the shade of an apple tree.*
2 A shade is something that partly covers a light to stop it shining in your eyes.

shadow A shadow is a dark shape that is made when something stands between a light and a surface.

shake
1 If you shake something you move it quickly up and down or backwards and forwards.
2 If something shakes, it moves quickly from side to side or up and down: *When the lorry went by outside, the table shook.*

shallow (shallower, shallowest) Something such as a hole or a container that is shallow measures only a short distance from top to bottom.

shame is an unhappy feeling that people have when they have done something wrong.

shampoo is a soapy liquid that you use for washing your hair.

shape The shape of something is the way its outside edges look; for example, whether they are straight or curved.

share
1 If you share something with another person, you both have the use of it: *She went up to the bedroom she shared with her sister.*
2 If you share something between a group of people, you divide it so that everyone gets some.

shark A shark is a very large fish that lives in the sea. It has sharp teeth. Some sharks attack people.

sharp (sharper, sharpest)
1 A sharp object has a very thin edge that is good for cutting things.
2 Sharp can also mean finely pointed. For example, pins and needles are sharp.

shave When a man shaves he cuts hair from his face. He uses a razor or shaver so that he can get very close to his skin.

shed A shed is a small building, often made of wood. It is used for storing things such as garden tools.

sheep A sheep is a farm animal with a thick woolly coat. Sheep are usually kept for their wool or their meat.

sheet
1 A sheet is a large piece of thin cloth such as cotton, which is put on the bed.
2 A sheet of something such as paper or glass is a rectangular piece of it.

shelf A shelf is something flat which is fixed to a wall or inside a cupboard.

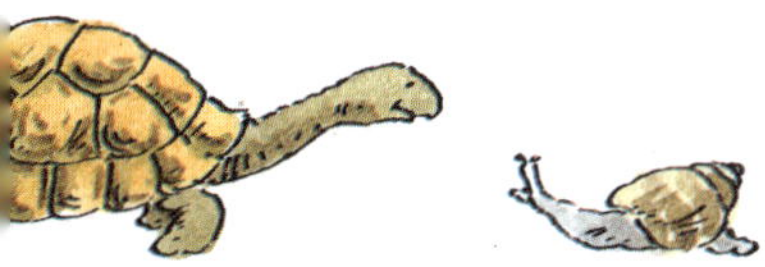

shell
1 The shell of an egg or nut is the hard covering round it.
2 The shell of an animal such as a tortoise or snail is the hard covering that it has on its back.
3 If you shell something such as peas or nuts you take their covering off.

shellfish A shellfish is any small sea creature that has a shell. Prawns and crabs are shellfish.

shelter A shelter is a small building or covered place where people or animals can be safe from bad weather or danger.

shield A shield is a large piece of metal or leather which soldiers used to carry: *They used the shields to protect themselves from injury when they were fighting.*

shine
1 When something shines, it gives out bright light.
2 If you make an object shine, you make it bright by rubbing or polishing it.

ship A ship is a large boat which sails across the sea.

shirt A shirt is a piece of clothing worn on the top part of your body.

shiver When you shiver, your body shakes slightly, usually because you are cold or frightened.

shock A shock is a sudden, nasty surprise.

shoe Shoes are objects that you wear to cover your feet.

shoot
1 A shoot is a new part growing from a plant or tree.
2 To shoot means to fire a bullet from a gun, or to fire an arrow from a bow.
3 If someone shoots in a game such as football, they try to score a goal.

shop A shop is a building or part of a building where things are sold.

shore The shore of a sea or lake is the land along the edge of it.

short (shorter, shortest)
1 If something lasts for a short time, it does not last very long.
2 Someone who is short is not as tall as most other people.
3 Something that is short is not very long.

shorts are short trousers.

shoulder Your shoulder is the place where your arm joins on to your body.

shout
1 A shout is a loud call or cry.
2 If you shout, you say words as loudly as you can.

show
1 A show is a kind of entertainment at the theatre or on television.
2 A show is also a kind of competition in which a judge decides who is best at something. There are shows for things such as flowers, dogs and cattle.
3 If you show somebody something, you let them see it.

shower (say shour)
1 A shower is a short period of light rain.
2 A shower is also a piece of equipment in the bathroom. It gives out a fine spray of water so that you can wash yourself.

shriek If you shriek, you give a sudden sharp cry. This is usually because you are excited, or in pain.

shrimp A shrimp is a small grey shellfish. It has a long tail and a pair of pincers. It turns pink when it is cooked.

shut
1 If you shut something such as a door, you move it so that it fills a gap.
2 If you shut your eyes, you lower your lids so that you cannot see.
3 If you shut your mouth, you put your lips together.
4 If a place such as a shop shuts it is closed. You cannot go in until it is open again.

shy A shy person is someone who is afraid to meet or speak to anyone they do not know.

sick If you are sick, you are not well.

side
1 The side of something is to the left or right of it: *He parted his hair on the left side.*
2 The side of something is the edge of it: *There is a fence on three sides of the garden.*
3 The sides of a river or lake are its banks.
4 The sides of a hill are the sloping parts between the top and bottom.
5 The sides of a piece of paper are its front and back: *What does it say on the other side?*
6 The two sides in a game are the teams playing against each other.

sideboard A sideboard is a large piece of dining room furniture. Sideboards have cupboards and drawers to hold things such as plates and knives and forks. .

sigh When you sigh you breathe out heavily. People usually sigh when they are tired or bored.

sight is the ability to see.

sign
1 A sign is a mark or shape that means something. For example, a plus sign.
2 A sign is also a piece of something such as wood or metal with words or pictures on it.
3 If you sign something, you write your name on it.

silence If there is silence, it is quiet because nobody is speaking.

silk is a thread spun by silkworms. It is made into fine, smooth cloth.

silly If someone says you are silly, they mean you are behaving in a foolish or childish way.

silver is a valuable greyish-white metal. It is used for making jewellery and ornaments.

similar If something is similar to something else, the two things are rather alike.

simple (simpler, simplest) If something is simple, it is easy to do or understand.

sing
1 If you sing a song you make music with your voice. Usually people sing words that fit the music.
2 When birds sing, the sounds they make are like music.

single means one of something: *We can't park here. It's a single yellow line.*

sink
1 A sink is a large basin in a kitchen. Sinks have water taps and a drain.
2 If something sinks it moves slowly downwards, especially into water.

sip If you sip a drink, you drink it a little at a time.

siren A siren is something that makes a loud wailing noise as a warning. Fire engines, police cars and ambulances have sirens.

sit
1 When you sit, you seat yourself on something such as a chair or the floor.
2 When a bird sits on its eggs, it covers them with its body to hatch them.

size The size of something is how big or small it is.

skate
1 A skate is a special boot that you wear to ice-skate or roller-skate.
2 A skate is also a very flat sea fish. It has two large fins like wings.

skateboard A skateboard is a narrow board with four wheels. You can stand on it and ride about.

skeleton The skeleton of a person or animal is all the bones that support the body.

ski Skis are long flat narrow pieces of wood, metal or plastic.

skid If a vehicle skids it slides sideways while it is moving along. This is usually because the road is slippery.

skilful Someone who is skilful at something does it very well.

skill is the ability to do something very well.

skin
1 Your skin is the natural covering of your body.
2 The skin of a fruit or vegetable is its outer layer or covering.

skip
1 When you skip, you move along almost as though you were dancing, with little jumps.
2 If you skip with a rope, you swing the rope over your head and under your feet.

skirt A skirt is a piece of clothing worn by women and girls. It hangs from the waist.

skull Your skull is the bony part of your head. It has your brain inside it.

sky The sky is the space around the earth which you can see when you stand outside and look upwards.

skyscraper A skyscraper is a very tall building.

slam If you slam a door you shut it hard so that it makes a loud noise.

slate is a dark grey rock that splits easily into thin layers. It is often used for roofs.

sledge A sledge is a vehicle for travelling on snow.

sleep When you sleep, you close your eyes and your whole body rests.

sleet is rain that is partly frozen as it falls.

sleeve The sleeves of a coat or other piece of clothing are the parts that cover your arms.

slice A slice is a piece of food that has been cut from a larger piece: *Can I have a slice of cake, please?*

slide
1 A slide is a small piece of film in a frame. It has a picture on it.
2 A slide is also a piece of playground equipment.
3 When something slides, it moves smoothly over a surface.

slight (slighter, slightest) Something that is slight is very small: *She has a slight cut.*

slim (slimmer, slimmest) Someone who is slim has a thin body.

slip
1 A slip is a small mistake.
2 If you slip, you accidentally slide and lose your balance.

slippers are loose, soft shoes that people wear in the house.

slope A slope is ground that goes up or down.

slot A slot is a narrow opening in a machine or container. For example, public telephones have slots to put money or cards in.

slow (slower, slowest)
1 Something that is slow moves along without much speed.
2 If a clock or watch is slow, it shows a time that is earlier than the correct time.

smack If a person smacks someone, they hit them with an open hand.

small (smaller, smallest) Something that is small is not as large as other things of the same kind: *A baby is small compared with its mother.*

smash If something smashes, it falls and hits the ground. It makes a loud noise and breaks into lots of pieces.

smell When you smell something, you notice it with your nose.

smile When you smile, the corners of your mouth move upwards and you look happy.

smoke is made up of clouds of gas and small bits of solid material. Smoke goes into the air when something is burning.

smooth (smoother, smoothest)
1 A smooth surface has no roughness, lumps or holes.
2 A smooth liquid or mixture does not have any lumps in it.
3 A smooth ride is one that is comfortable because there are no bumps or jerks.

smuggler A smuggler is a person who takes things in or out of a country when it is against the law.

snack A snack is a small, quick meal. For example, a sandwich is a snack.

snail A snail is a small, slow-moving creature. It has a shell on its back.

snake A snake is a long, thin reptile. It has scales on its skin and no legs.

snap
1 A snap is a photograph.
2 Snap is a card game played by children.
3 If something snaps, it breaks suddenly. It usually makes a sharp cracking noise.

snatch If you snatch something, you take it quickly and suddenly.

sneeze When you sneeze, you take in your breath and blow it down your nose suddenly.

sniff If you sniff, you breathe in through your nose hard enough to make a sound.

snore When people snore, they breathe very noisily when they are sleeping.

snorkel A snorkel is an air tube that swimmers sometimes use. One end stays above the water so that a person swimming under water can breathe.

snow is frozen water that falls from the sky as snowflakes in cold weather.

soak When liquid soaks something, it makes it very wet: *The rain soaked right through my coat.*

soap is a solid, liquid or powder that you use with water for washing.

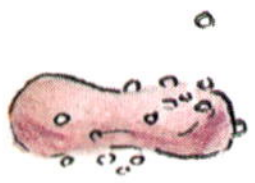

soccer is a game of football played with a round ball.

sock A sock is a soft piece of clothing which covers your foot and ankle.

sofa A sofa is a long, comfortable seat for more than one person.

soft (softer, softest)
1 Something that is soft changes shape easily when you touch it.
2 A soft sound or voice is quiet and gentle.
3 A soft light or colour is pleasant and restful because it is not too bright.

soil
1 Soil is the top layer of earth which plants can grow in.
2 If you soil something, you make it dirty.

soldier A soldier is a person in an army.

sole
1 The sole of your foot is the underneath surface of it.
2 A sole is the underneath of a shoe or sock.
3 A sole is also a flat sea fish.

solid Something that is solid stays the same shape whether it is in a container or not. Things that are solid are usually also firm or hard. Metal, wood and rock are all solid.

song A song is a piece of music with words.

soon (sooner, soonest) Soon means in the very near future.

soot is black powder which comes from burning coal or wood.

sore If part of your body is sore, it is painful: *Her throat was so sore she couldn't talk.*

sorry
1 You say you are sorry to someone if you have upset them.
2 If you feel sorry about something that has happened, you feel disappointed or sad: *I was sorry to leave all my friends.*
3 If you feel sorry for someone, you feel sad for them.

sort
1 Sort means kind or type.
2 All sorts of things means lots of different things.
3 If you sort things, you put them into groups: *Can you sort your socks into pairs?*

sound A sound is something that you hear.

soup is a liquid food. It is made by boiling things such as meat or vegetables in water.

sour
1 Something that is sour tastes sharp.
2 If milk is sour, it is no longer fresh.

south is one of the four main compass points. If you face the point where the sun rises, south is on your right.

sow (as in go) If you sow seeds, you plant them in the ground so that they will grow.

space
1 Space is the area in something such as a building or container that is empty: *There is just enough space for a bed and a chair in my room.*
2 Space is also the place far above the earth where there is no air.

spaceship A spaceship is a rocket or other vehicle that can travel in space.

spade A spade is a tool used for digging. It has a flat metal blade and a long handle.

spark
1 A spark is a tiny piece of very bright burning material. A spark can fly up from something burning. It can also be caused by two hard things hitting against each other.
2 A spark is also a flash of light caused by electricity.

sparkle If something sparkles, it gives off little flashes of light.

sparrow A sparrow is a small brown bird. It is very common in Britain and many other countries.

speak
1 When you speak, you use your voice to say words.
2 If you speak a foreign language, you know the language: *Can you speak French?*

spear A spear is a weapon. It is made from a long pole with a sharp metal point at one end.

special
1 Something that is special is more important or better than other things of its kind.
2 Special can also mean something that is made for a particular use: *You need a special tool to do this job.*

speck A speck is a tiny piece of something: *There wasn't a speck of dust anywhere.*

speech
1 Speech is the ability to speak.
2 A speech is a talk that someone gives when something special is happening. For example, the bride's father usually makes a speech at a wedding.

speed
1 The speed of something is how fast or slowly it travels: *What speed does a snail travel?*
2 Speed can be used to talk about how fast or slowly something happens: *My two children are growing at different speeds.*
3 Speed is also very fast movement.

spell
1 In fairy stories, a spell is words that have a magic power.
2 When you spell a word, you write or say the letters in the right order.

spend
1 When you spend money, you pay out the money for things that you want.
2 If you spend time doing something, you use that amount of time doing it: *I spend hours playing soccer.*

sphere A sphere is an object or a shape that is like a ball.

spider A spider is a small creature with eight legs. Most kinds of spider make webs. They use the webs to catch insects for food.

spike A spike is a long piece of metal with a sharp point at one end.

spin

1 If something spins, it turns round and round quickly.

2 When someone spins thread, they pull out threads of cotton or wool and twist them together very quickly.

3 When a spider spins a web, it makes it from a silky thread that comes out of its body.

spine Your spine is the row of bones down your back that holds your body up.

splash

1 If you splash, you throw water about.

2 A splash is the sound that is made when something hits the water.

splendid Something that is splendid is excellent and of very good quality.

split If something such as wood or a piece of clothing splits, a long crack or tear appears in it.

spoil

1 If you spoil something, you make it less enjoyable than it would have been.

2 If someone spoils an object they damage it.

3 If someone spoils a child, they give them all their own way.

spoke Spokes are the bars that join the rim of a wheel to its centre.

sponge A sponge is a sea creature with a soft round body. The skeleton of a sponge is full of holes and can hold a lot of water. You can use it to wash with. This is called natural sponge. There is a similar factory-made sponge.

spoon A spoon is a tool shaped like a small shallow bowl with a long handle. It is used for eating, mixing and serving food.

sport Sports are games such as football and cricket, which need energy and skill. In most sports, the players are organized in teams. Each team tries to win.

spot

1 A spot is a round area on a surface. Some fabrics have patterns of spots.

2 A spot can be a particular place: *This would be a nice spot for a picnic.*

spout A spout is a special shaped opening or tube in a container. It allows liquids to be poured easily.

spray is a lot of tiny drops of liquid, forced from something such as a hose or a spray can.

spread

1 If you spread something, you arrange it over a surface: *They spread their wet clothes out to dry.*

2 If you spread something such as butter, you put a thin layer of it on to something.

3 If you spread parts of your body such as your arms, you stretch them out until they are far apart.

spring

1 Spring is the season between winter and summer. Plants begin to grow in the spring.

2 A spring is a curled piece of wire.

3 A spring is also a pool that forms where water comes up through the ground.

sprint A sprint is a short, fast race.

sprout
1 Sprouts are small green vegetables which look like very small cabbages.
2 When plants sprout, they put out new leaves or shoots.

spy
1 A spy is a person whose job is to find out secret information about another country or organisation.
2 If you spy something, you notice it.

square
1 A square is a shape which has four straight sides all the same length.
2 A square is also a flat open place in a town or city.

squash
1 Squash is a ball game played between two people.
2 Squash is also a fruit drink.
3 If you squash something you press it, so that it goes flat: *She put her bag on the tomatoes, and squashed them.*

squeeze When you squeeze something, you press it firmly on all sides.

squirrel A squirrel is a small furry animal with a long, bushy tail. It eats things such as nuts and seeds. Squirrels usually live in trees. A squirrel's nest is called a drey.

stable A stable is a building in which horses are kept.

stack A stack is a number of things arranged in a neat pile; for example, a stack of books.

stage A stage is a raised platform in a theatre or hall. Stages are often used for plays or other entertainment.

stagecoach A stagecoach is a large carriage pulled by horses. Stagecoaches used to carry passengers and mail.

stain A stain is a mark which is difficult to remove.

stairs are a set of steps, usually inside a building. You use them to walk up or down to a different level.

stale (staler, stalest) something which is stale is no longer fresh.

stalk
1 A stalk is the main stem of a plant.
2 A stalk is also the part of a plant that joins the flowers, fruit and leaves to the main stem.

stamp
1 A stamp is a small piece of gummed paper, usually with a picture on it.
2 If you stamp your foot, you lift your foot and suddenly put it down very hard. Some children stamp their foot if they are cross.

stand
1 A stand is an open building at a sports ground. People can sit or stand there in rows to watch what is happening.
2 When you stand, your body is upright and you are on your feet.

star
1 A star is a large natural object in space. Stars can be seen as tiny points of light in the sky at night.
2 A star is also a shape with a number of sharp points.
3 A star can also be a very successful person in sport or entertainment.

stare If you stare, you look at someone or something for a long time with wide open eyes.

starling A starling is a very common European bird. It has greenish-black feathers. Starlings live and fly in large groups.

start
1 When you start to do something, you begin doing it.
2 If someone starts an engine, they make it begin to work.

startle If something startles you, it frightens you by making a sudden movement or noise.

starve When people or animals starve they suffer greatly from lack of food. They sometimes die.

station
1 A station is a building where trains or buses stop for passengers.
2 A station is also a building which is used by people such as the police or the fire brigade.

statue A statue is a large sculpture of a person or animal. Statues are usually made from stone or metal.

steady (steadier, steadiest) If something such as a ladder is steady, it is firm and does not move about.

steal If someone steals something, they take away something that belongs to someone else, without permission.

steam is the hot mist that water turns into when it boils.

steel is a very strong metal, made mostly from iron.

steep (steeper, steepest) Something such as a road or hill that is steep slopes very sharply.

steer When someone steers something like a car or cycle, they make it go in the direction they want.

stem
1 The stem of a plant is the long thin centre part.
2 A stem is also one of the smaller parts of a plant which hold leaves, flowers or fruit.

step
1 A step is the movement you make when you lift your foot and put it down in a different place.
2 A step is also a raised flat surface like a block. There are often two or more steps together.

stick
1 A stick is a long, thin piece of wood.
2 A stick of something is a long, thin piece of it: *I need a few sticks of rhubarb.*
3 If you stick a pointed object such as a drawing pin into something, you push it in.
4 If you stick two things together, you fix them with something like glue or tape.
5 If something such as a drawer sticks, it cannot be moved.

stiff (stiffer, stiffest) Something that is stiff is quite hard or firm. It will not bend very much if it is pressed: *Use a stiff broom to sweep up the leaves.*

stile A stile is a kind of fixed gate with a step each side. It is made so that people can get into a field without letting animals out.

sting The sting of an insect or plant is the part that can prick someone's skin and leave poison behind.

stir If you stir a liquid you mix it inside a container. You move something such as a spoon round and round in it.

stitch If you stitch fabric, you push a needle and thread in and out through it.

stocking Stockings are two pieces of clothing worn by women to cover their feet and legs.

stomach Your stomach is the part of your body that holds food when you have eaten it.

stone
1 Stone is a hard, dry material that is dug out of the ground. It is often used for building houses and walls.
2 A stone is a small piece of rock which you find on the surface of the ground.
3 A jewel is sometimes called a stone.
4 A stone is also a large, hard seed which grows in the middle of some kinds of fruit. For example, peaches and plums have stones in them.

stool A stool is a seat. It has legs, but no back.

stop If you stop what you are doing, you no longer do it.

store
1 A store is a large shop which sells a lot of different things.
2 When you store things you put them away and keep them until they are wanted.

stork A stork is a large bird with a long beak and long legs. Storks usually live near water.

storm A storm is very bad weather with heavy rain and strong winds. Often there is thunder and lightning.

story A story is a tale about something that has happened. It can be about something real, or something made up.

straight (straighter, straightest) Something such as a line that is straight does not bend or curve.

strange (stranger, strangest)
1 Something that is strange is odd or unexpected.
2 A strange place is one you have never been to before.

stranger A stranger is a person you do not know or have never met before.

straw
1 Straw is dried stalks of cereal such as wheat. Straw can be used for animals to sleep on.
2 A straw is a thin tube made of paper or plastic. You can use a straw to suck drink into your mouth.

strawberry A strawberry is a small red fruit. It is soft and juicy, and has tiny yellow seeds on its skin.

stream A stream is a small river.

street A street is a road in a town or village. It has buildings along it, often with a pavement on each side.

strength
1 Your strength is your ability to move or lift things.
2 The strength of a wind or a water current is its force and the speed it moves.

stretch
1 A stretch of land or water is an area of land or water.
2 If you stretch, you pull your arms or legs stiffly away from your body.

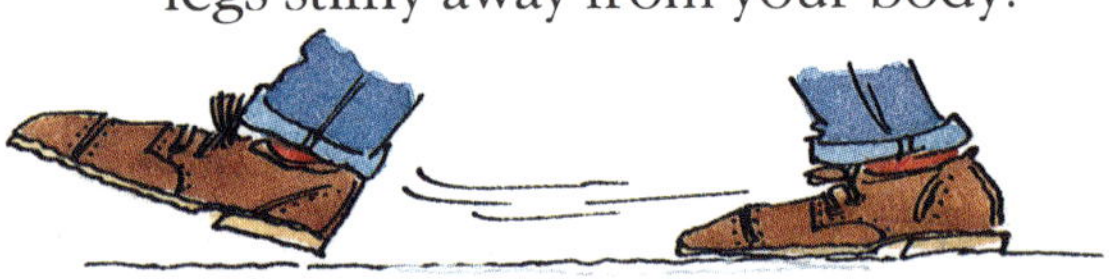

stride A stride is a long step which you take when you are walking or running.

strike
1 If you strike something you hit it.
2 When a clock strikes, its bells make a sound to show what the time is.
3 If someone strikes a match, they make a flame or sparks with the match.

string String is thin cord made of twisted threads. It is used for tying things together.

stroke If you stroke something such as an animal, you move your hand slowly and gently over it.

strong (stronger, strongest)
1 People or animals that are strong can work hard and carry heavy things.
2 Objects or materials that are strong will not break easily.

study
1 A study is a room which is used for reading and writing.
2 If you study something, you spend time learning about it.
3 If you study an object such as a map or a picture, you look at it very carefully.

stumble If you stumble when you are walking, you trip and almost fall.

stupid (stupider, stupidest)
Someone who is stupid does things that are not at all sensible.

subject
1 A subject is a particular thing that people study at school or college; for example, science or drawing.
2 If you change the subject when you are talking to someone, you suddenly talk about something different.

submarine A submarine is a ship that can travel under water.

subway A subway is a tunnel under a road. People can use it to get to the other side of a road safely.

success is managing to do something that you set out to do.

suck If you suck something, you draw liquid from it into your mouth.

sudden Something that is sudden happens quickly and unexpectedly.

sugar is a sweet food which you usually buy in crystal form. It is used to sweeten other foods and drinks. Sugar comes from sugar beet or sugar cane.

suit
1 A suit is a set of clothes made from the same material. A suit usually has a jacket and trousers, and sometimes a waistcoat.
2 If a piece of clothing suits you, you look nice in it.

suitable Something that is suitable for a particular purpose is right for it: *You can't wear those shoes for running. They're not suitable.*

sultana A sultana is a dried white grape.

sum
1 A sum is an amount of money.
2 A sum is also a problem in arithmetic.

summer is the season between spring and autumn. In the summer the weather is usually warmer and drier than it is during other seasons.

sun The sun is the ball of fire in the sky that the earth goes round. It gives us light and heat.

Sunday is one of the seven days of the week. It is the day after Saturday and before Monday.

sunflower A sunflower is a very tall plant. It has a large flat flower with yellow petals and a brown centre.

supermarket A supermarket is a large shop which sells all kinds of food and things for the house.

supersonic speeds are greater than the speed of sound.

supper is an evening meal.

supply If someone supplies you with something, they give it or sell it to you.

support
1 If something supports an object, it holds it up firmly.
2 If someone supports a sports team, they go regularly to their games.

sure (surer, surest) If you are sure that something is true, you believe it is true.

surf is the large waves that break on the shore.

surface The surface of something is the outside or top part of it.

surgery A surgery is the place where a doctor or dentist sees their patients.

surprise A surprise is something unexpected.

surrender If someone surrenders, they stop fighting and agree that they have lost.

swallow
1 A swallow is a small dark blue and white bird. Swallows catch insects as they fly.
2 When you swallow food or drink, it goes down your throat into your stomach.

swamp A swamp is an area of very wet land.

swan A swan is a large bird with a long neck. It lives on rivers and lakes.

swarm A swarm is a large group of bees or other insects flying together.

sweat (say swet) Sweat is the salty liquid which comes from your skin when you are hot.

sweater A sweater is a warm knitted garment. You put on a sweater by pulling it over your head.

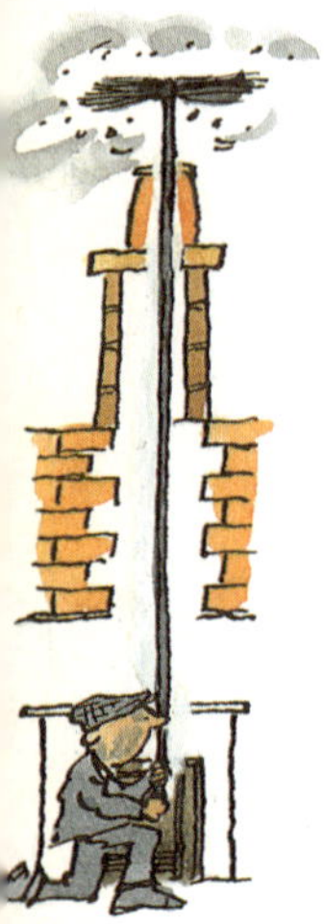

sweep
1 A sweep is someone who cleans chimneys.
2 If you sweep a floor or a path, you clean it by pushing a broom over it.

sweet (sweeter, sweetest)
1 Food or drink that is sweet has sugar in it, or tastes as though it has sugar in it.
2 Sweets are things such as chocolate and toffees.
3 A sweet can be something such as yoghurt or fruit salad that is eaten after the main part of a meal.

swell If something swells, it becomes larger and rounder than usual.

swerve If something that is moving swerves, it suddenly changes direction.

swift (swifter, swiftest)
1 A swift is a small black-brown bird. It has curved wings and a forked tail. Swifts make a loud noise like a scream. They fly very quickly and catch insects while they are flying.
2 Something that is swift can move very quickly.

swim When you swim, you move through water by making movements with your arms and legs.

swing A swing is a seat that hangs from two ropes or chains. A child can sit on the seat and move forwards and backwards.

switch A switch is a small control for a piece of electrical equipment such as a light or radio.

sword (say sord) A sword is a weapon with a long blade. It has a handle at one end.

symbol A symbol is a shape or a pattern that means something. For example, + is a symbol. It means you have to add two numbers together.

syrup
1 Syrup is a sweet, fairly thick liquid. It is made by cooking sugar with water.
2 Syrup is also a very sweet, sticky liquid food. For example, golden syrup.

table A table is a piece of furniture. It has a flat top for putting things on.

tadpole Tadpoles are small water creatures that grow into frogs or toads. They have long tails and round black heads.

tail
1 A tail is the part of an animal, bird or fish that grows out of the end of its body.
2 A tail is also a long part of something which sticks out from the end. For example, the tail of a kite.

tale A tale is a story, especially one about adventure or magic.

talk
1 When you talk, you use words so that people will understand you.
2 If something can talk, it makes noises that sound like a human being talking: *My parrot can talk.*

tall
1 Someone who is tall is higher than a lot of other people: *My father is very tall. He is over two metres.*
2 Something that is tall is higher than other things of the same kind: *At the end of the street there is a tall building.*

tambourine A tambourine is a musical instrument. It is a small hand drum with jingling metal discs all round the edge.

tame (tamer, tamest) A tame animal or bird is one which is not afraid of humans and will not hurt them.

tank
1 A tank is a large container for liquid or gas.
2 A tank is also a vehicle for soldiers. Tanks are covered with strong metal armour, and have guns or rockets.

tanker A tanker is a ship, truck or railway vehicle for carrying gas or liquid.

tap
1 A tap is a handle fixed to a pipe or container. It controls the flow of gas or liquid.
2 If you tap something, you hit it gently.

tape
1 Tape is long thin magnetic strip that will record sounds or pictures.
2 Tape is also a long narrow strip of cloth. Tapes are used to tie things together, or to put names on clothes.
3 Some tape is sticky. It is made from thin paper or plastic, and has one sticky side. You can use it to stick things such as pieces of paper together.

tar is a thick, black liquid that goes hard when it is cold. Tar is used mainly for making roads.

target A target is an object that people aim at when they are shooting. It is usually a board with circles marked on it.

tart A tart is a piece of pastry filled with jam or fruit.

taste is one of the five senses that people and animals have. It is your sense of taste that lets you know what you are eating or drinking.

taxi A taxi is a car that people pay to ride in.

tea
1 Tea is a drink. It is made by pouring boiling water on to the dried leaves of the tea plant.
2 Tea is also a meal in the afternoon or early evening.

teach If someone teaches you something, they tell you how to do it.

team A team is a number of people or animals working or playing together.

teapot A teapot is a container for making and serving tea. It has a lid, a handle and a spout.

tear (as in air) If someone tears something such as paper or fabric, they pull it apart.

tear (as in ear) Tears are the drops of salty liquid that come out of your eyes when you cry.

tease If someone teases you they make fun of you.

teaspoon a teaspoon is a small spoon that you use to put sugar into tea or coffee.

teenager A teenager is someone between 13 and 19 years of age.

telescope A telescope is an instrument for making objects that are far away look nearer and larger.

television A television is a piece of electrical equipment. With a television people can watch programmes of pictures and sounds that have come through the air.

tell
1 If you tell someone something, you give them information about it.
2 If someone tells you to do something, they say you must do it.
3 If you can tell the time, you can find out what the time is by looking at a clock or watch.

temper Someone's temper is how cheerful or how angry they are feeling at a particular time.

temperature The temperature is the amount of heat there is in a place. In hot countries, the temperature is very high. Temperatures can be measured.

tender
1 Someone who is tender is gentle and caring.
2 Meat or other food that is tender is very soft and easy to cut.
3 If part of your body is tender, it hurts when you touch it.

tennis is a ball game for two or four players.

tent A tent is a shelter made of canvas or nylon. It is held up by poles and ropes. People sleep in a tent when they are camping.

term A term is one of the periods that schools and colleges divide the year into. In Britain there are usually three terms in a year.

terrible You say something is terrible when you think it is very bad or unpleasant.

terrify If something terrifies you it makes you feel very frightened.

terror is very great fear.

test
1 A test is something you have to do, to show how much you know.
2 If someone tests something, they try to find out whether it works properly.

thank
1 You thank people when you are grateful for something they have done or said.
2 You say thank you when you take or refuse something: *Would you like some more potato? – No, thank you.*

thaw When something that is frozen thaws, it melts.

theatre A theatre is a building with a stage in it. People go to the theatre to watch plays and other entertainments.

thermometer A thermometer is an instrument for measuring how hot or cold something is.

thick (thicker, thickest)
1 An object that is thick is deeper through than other things of the same kind: *I should like a thick slice of bread, please.*
2 Something that is thick is made up of a lot of things growing closely together: *She found herself in a thick forest.*
3 Liquids that are thick do not flow easily.
4 Something such as smoke or fog that is thick is difficult to see through.

thimble A thimble is a small metal or plastic object that you put on your finger when you are sewing. The thimble helps you push the needle through the cloth.

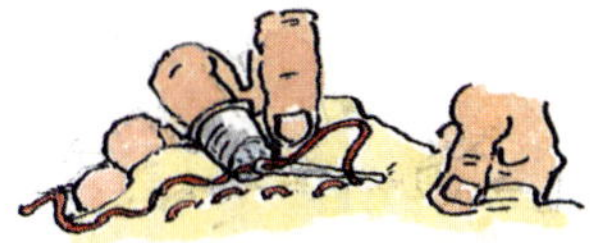

thin (thinner, thinnest)
1 Something that is thin is much narrower than it is long: *The witch's nose was long and thin.*
2 A person that is thin weighs less than most other people.

think
1 If you say you think something is true, you mean you believe it is true, but you are not sure.
2 If you are thinking about something, you have words or ideas in your mind.

thirsty (thirstier, thirstiest) If you feel thirsty, you feel that you need to drink something.

thistle A thistle is a wild plant. It has prickly leaves and purple flowers.

thorn A thorn is one of the sharp points on the stem of a plant such as a rose.

thread is a long, very thin piece of material such as cotton, wool, silk or nylon. Thread can be woven into cloth. It can also be used for sewing fabrics together.

thrill A thrill is a sudden feeling of great excitement or pleasure.

throat Your throat is the back of your mouth and inside your neck. It contains the tubes for breathing and for swallowing food.

throw If you throw an object that you are holding, you send the object through the air.

thrush A thrush is a songbird. It has a brown back and a pale spotted chest.

thumb Your thumb is one of the five fingers on your hand. It is the finger which is nearest to your wrist.

thunder is the loud noise that you hear after a flash of lightning in a storm.

Thursday is one of the seven days of the week. It is the day after Wednesday and before Friday.

tick A tick is a sign to show that something is correct.

ticket A ticket is a small piece of card or paper that shows you have paid for something such as a train ride.

tickle
1 A tickle is an unpleasant and annoying feeling somewhere on your body. If you have a tickle in your throat it makes you want to cough.
2 If you tickle somebody, you move your fingers gently on part of their body, to make them laugh.

tide The tide is the regular change in the level of the sea on the shore. There are two high tides and two low tides every day.

tidy (tidier, tidiest) Something that is tidy is neat, with things in their proper place.

tie
1 A tie is a long narrow piece of cloth that is worn round the neck.
2 A tie is also a result in a race or competition when two people do as well as each other.
3 If you tie an object to something else, you fasten it with something such as string.
4 If you tie something such as shoelaces, you fasten the ends together into a bow.

tiger A tiger is a large, fierce animal that belongs to the cat family. Tigers live in Asia. Their fur is usually orange with black stripes.

tight (tighter, tightest)
1 Clothes that are tight fit closely to your body. Tight clothes are often uncomfortable.
2 If you hold something tight, you hold it very firmly.
3 Something that is tight is firmly fastened and is difficult to move.
4 Something that is shut tight is shut very firmly.

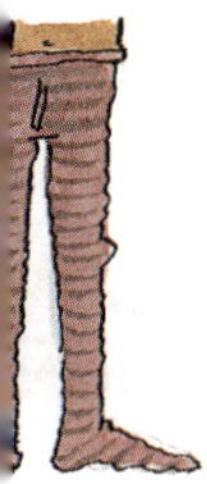

tights are a piece of clothing made of thin, stretchy material. They fit closely round a person's feet and legs, and round the lower part of their body.

timber is wood that is used for things such as building and making furniture.

time is what we measure in units such as hours, days and years.

timid A person or animal that is timid is shy and easily frightened.

tin
1 Tin is a silvery-white metal.
2 A tin is a metal container. It is filled with food and sealed. This preserves the food for long periods.
3 A tin is also a metal container with a lid, for storing things such as biscuits.
4 A cake tin is a metal container used for baking cakes in an oven.

tinkle If something tinkles, it makes a sound like a small bell ringing.

tinsel is made from long pieces of thread with small shiny strips fixed to them. Tinsel is used as a decoration.

tiny (tinier, tiniest) Something that is tiny is very small.

tip
1 The tip of something long and narrow is the end of it: *The cat caught the tip of its tail in the door.*
2 If you tip an object, you move it so that it is no longer straight: *She tipped her chair back and almost fell over.*
3 If you tip something somewhere, you pour it quickly.

tiptoe If you tiptoe somewhere, you walk there very quietly on your toes.

tired If you are tired, you feel that you want to rest or sleep.

tissue
1 Tissue is thin paper that is used especially for wrapping things such as objects made of glass or china.
2 A tissue is a piece of soft paper that you can use as a handkerchief. It can be thrown away after use.

title
1 The title of something such as a book is the name given to it by the person who wrote it.
2 Someone's title is a name such as Mr, Mrs, Lady, or Professor, that goes in front of their own name.

toad A toad is a creature which is similar to a frog. It has drier skin than a frog, and does not spend so much time in the water. Toads walk. They do not leap as frogs do.

toadstool A toadstool is a poisonous plant that looks like a mushroom.

toast is bread which has been cut into slices and made brown and crisp by heating.

today is the day that is happening now.

toddler A toddler is a small child who has only just learned to walk.

toe Your toes are the five moveable parts at the end of your foot.

toffee is a sticky, chewy sweet made from butter and sugar.

toilet A toilet is the same as a lavatory.

tomato A tomato is a soft, small red fruit.

tomorrow is the day after today.

tongue
1 Your tongue is the soft moving part inside your mouth. You use your tongue for tasting, eating and speaking.
2 The tongue of a shoe or boot is the piece of material underneath the laces.

tonight is the evening of today, or the night that follows today.

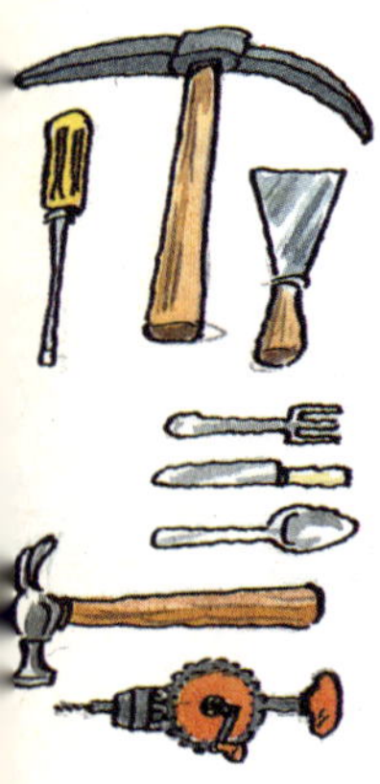

tonne A tonne is a measure of weight. It is equal to 1000 kilograms.

tool A tool is any instrument or piece of equipment that you hold in your hands to help you do something. For example, knives and forks, hammers and screwdrivers are all tools.

tooth

1 A tooth is one of the hard white objects which grow in your mouth. You use your teeth for biting and chewing food.
2 The teeth of objects such as combs, saws and zips are the parts that stick out in a row on their edge.

toothbrush A toothbrush is a small brush with a long handle. You use it for cleaning your teeth.

toothpaste is a thick paste which you put on your toothbrush to clean your teeth.

top
1 The top of something is its highest point.
2 The top of something such as a bottle or tube is the lid or cap that fits onto the end of it.

torch A torch is a small lamp which you carry in your hand. It gets its power from batteries inside it.

tortoise A tortoise is a slow-moving animal with a hard, thick shell. It can pull its legs and head inside the shell to protect itself.

toss If you toss something you throw it into the air.

touch
1 If you touch something, you feel it with your hand.
2 If two things are touching, there is no space between them.

tough (tougher, toughest)
1 Someone who is tough is very strong, and is not afraid of pain.
2 Material that is tough is strong. It is difficult to cut, tear or break.

tow If a vehicle tows another vehicle, it pulls it along behind.

towel A towel is a piece of thick, soft cloth that you use to dry yourself with.

tower A tower is a tall, narrow building or part of a building. Many churches and castles have towers.

town A town is a place with a lot of streets and buildings where people live and work. Towns are larger than villages and smaller than cities.

toy A toy is an object that children play with; for example, a doll or a model car.

track
1 A track is a rough and narrow road or path. Some tracks are made by people or animals walking along them.
2 A track is also a special road or path that is used for racing.
3 A railway track is a long, narrow strip of ground with rails on either side. Trains travel along the rails.

tractor A tractor is a vehicle with large rear wheels. Tractors are used on farms for pulling or lifting things.

traffic is the movement of vehicles, on the road, in the air, or on water.

traffic lights are special signals to control the flow of traffic. Red lights mean stop. Green lights mean go.

traffic warden A traffic warden is a person whose job is to make sure that cars are parked properly.

trail
1 A trail is a rough path across open country or through woods.
2 A trail is also the scent, footprints and other signs that people and animals leave when they move along.

train
1 A train is a number of carriages or trucks which are joined together and pulled by an engine along a railway.
2 If someone trains you to do a job, they teach you the skills you need.
3 If you train a dog, you teach it to behave properly.

trainers are shoes that people wear for running or playing games.

trampoline A trampoline is a thing that is used to jump and bounce on. It is made of strong cloth held into a frame by springs.

transparent If something is transparent you can see through it. For example, glass is transparent.

transport is the moving of people and things from one place to another by vehicle.

trap A trap is an object that is specially made to catch animals.

trapdoor A trapdoor is a small door in a floor or ceiling.

trapeze A trapeze is a bar hung from a high place by ropes. People swing from trapezes in circuses.

travel
1 If you travel you go from one place to another, especially in foreign countries.
2 If something travels at a particular speed, it moves at that speed.

tray A tray is a flat piece of wood, metal or plastic with raised edges. It is used for carrying things such as food and drinks.

treacle is a thick, sweet, sticky liquid made from sugar.

treasure is a collection of valuable things such as jewels or paintings.

tree A tree is a large plant with a long trunk made of wood. Trees have branches and leaves.

tremble If you tremble, you shake slightly with small movements that you cannot control. People sometimes tremble if they are excited, frightened or ill.

triangle
1 A triangle is a shape which has three straight sides.
2 A triangle is also a musical instrument. It is made from a piece of metal shaped like a triangle. You play it by hitting it with a short metal bar.

trick
1 A trick is a clever or skilful act that someone does to entertain people.
2 If a person tricks someone, they deceive them.

tricycle A tricycle is a vehicle similar to a bicycle, but with three wheels.

trigger A trigger is a small lever on a gun. It is pulled to fire the gun.

trip
1 A trip is a journey to a place and back again.
2 If you trip, you knock your foot against something when you are walking and fall, or almost fall.

trouble
1 Troubles are things that cause worry.
2 If you have trouble doing something, you find it hard to do.

trousers are a piece of clothing. Trousers cover your legs and the lower part of your body.

trout A trout is a fairly large fish that lives in rivers and streams. There are several kinds of trout, and many of them are good to eat.

truck
1 A truck is a large motor vehicle which is open at the back. Trucks are used for carrying all sorts of loads.
2 A truck is also an open vehicle used for carrying things on a railway.

true (truer, truest)
1 If something is true, it is correct.
2 A true story is about something real that happened.

trumpet a trumpet is a brass musical instrument.

trunk
1 The trunk of a tree is its large main stem. Branches grow from the trunk.
2 Your trunk is the main part of your body.
3 An elephant's trunk is its very long nose. It uses its trunk to lift food and water and bring them to its mouth.
4 A trunk is also a large case or box with strong sides and a lid.

trust If you trust someone, you believe that they are honest. You are also sure they would not purposely do anything to hurt you.

try
1 If you try to do something, you do your best to do it.
2 If you try something, you test it to see what it is like.

tube
1 A tube is a long, hollow object like a pipe.
2 A tube is also a long, thin container for thick liquids or pastes such as toothpaste. You squeeze the tube to get the paste out of a hole in the end.
3 The tube is an underground railway in London.

Tuesday is one of the seven days of the week. It is the day after Monday and before Wednesday.

tug
1 a tug is a small, powerful boat which pulls large ships.
2 If you tug something you give it a quick, strong pull.

tulip A tulip is a brightly-coloured garden flower. It is shaped like an upside-down bell. Tulips grow from bulbs in the spring.

tumble If you tumble, you fall over and over.

tuna are large fish that live in warm seas. They are caught for food.

tune A tune is a series of musical notes. Tunes are usually nice to listen to and easy to remember.

tunnel A tunnel is a long passage which has been made under the ground or through a hill.

turban A turban is a head-covering worn by a Muslim, Hindu or Sikh man. It is made from a long piece of cloth wound round and round his head.

turkey A turkey is a large bird that is kept on a farm for its meat.

turnip A turnip is a round vegetable. It has a white, yellow or reddish skin. Turnips grow under the ground.

turtle A turtle is a large reptile with a thick shell. It spends most of its time in the sea.

tusk Tusks are long, pointed teeth that some animals have. For example, elephants and walruses have tusks.

twig A twig is a very small, thin branch of a tree or bush.

twilight is the time after sunset when it is just getting dark.

twin If two people or animals are twins, they have the same mother and were born on the same day.

twinkle If a star or light twinkles, it keeps changing from bright to dim.

twist When you twist something, you hold one end and turn the other end round and round.

type
1 Type means kind or sort: *What type of plant is it?*
2 If a person types something, they write it using something such as a typewriter.

typewriter A typewriter is a machine that prints words when you press keys with letters on them.

typhoon A typhoon is a storm with very strong winds.

tyre A tyre is a strong rubber ring fitted round a wheel. Tyres are usually filled with a lot of air. They are fitted to vehicles such as cars and bicycles.

ugly Someone or something that is ugly is not nice to look at.

umbrella An umbrella is a shelter from the rain. The top is made from thin cloth stretched over a light frame. It is fixed to a stick so that you can hold it over your head. You can close it when you are not using it.

unable If you are unable to do something, you cannot do it.

uncomfortable
1 If you are uncomfortable, you are not happy because you can feel a very slight pain.
2 If things such as clothes are uncomfortable, they do not feel right.

unconscious Someone who is unconscious is unable to see, hear or feel anything that is going on. This is usually because they have fainted or have been badly injured.

undercarriage The undercarriage of an aeroplane is the part with the wheels on.

underground
1 Something that is underground is below the surface of the ground.
2 In London, the Underground is a railway that runs in tunnels under the city.

understand If you understand something, you know what it means.

undo If you undo something that is fastened or tied together, you unfasten it.

undress When you undress, you take off your clothes.

uneven Something that is uneven has a bumpy surface.

unexpected Something that is unexpected surprises you.

unhappy (unhappier, unhappiest) Someone who is unhappy is sad or miserable.

unicorn A unicorn is an imaginary animal. It looks like a horse with a horn in the middle of its forehead.

uniform A uniform is a special set of clothes that is worn by people to show that they belong to the same group.

unit A unit is a fixed measure of something. For example, the second is a unit of time.

universe The universe is the whole of space and everything in it. The earth is part of the universe.

university A university is a place where people can carry on their education when they have left school.

unkind Someone who is unkind is rather cruel and unpleasant.

unload If people unload something such as a lorry, they take the load off it.

unlucky Someone who is unlucky has bad luck.

unnecessary Something that is unnecessary is not needed.

unpleasant
1 Someone who is unpleasant is not helpful or friendly.
2 Something that is unpleasant is rather nasty and not at all enjoyable.

unselfish People who are unselfish care more about other people than they do about themselves.

untidy (untidier, untidiest)
1 Someone who is untidy does not care whether things are neat and well arranged.
2 Somewhere or something that is untidy is messy and not well arranged.

unusual Someone or something that is unusual is different from the ordinary.

upset
1 If you are upset, you are unhappy or disappointed about something.
2 If someone upsets something, they turn it over by accident: *He upset a tin of paint on the carpet.*

urgent Something that is urgent needs to be done at once.

use If you use something such as a tool, you do something with it that helps you.

useful If something is useful, it helps you in some way.

useless If something is useless, you cannot use it.

usual Something that is usual is a thing that is nearly always done: *She got up earlier than usual.*

usually If something usually happens, it happens very often.

valley A valley is a low stretch of land between hills. Valleys quite often have rivers flowing through them.

valuable
1 Things such as jewellery or paintings that are valuable are worth a lot of money.
2 Help or advice that is valuable is very useful.

van A van is a covered truck. Vans are used to carry things from place to place.

vanish If something vanishes it disappears suddenly, or in a way that cannot be explained.

vase A vase is a kind of jar. Vases are usually made of glass or pottery. They are used to hold cut flowers, or as an ornament.

vegetable A vegetable is a plant which is eaten raw or cooked. For example, potatoes, cabbages and onions are vegetables.

vehicle A vehicle is a machine such as a car or bus that carries people or things from place to place.

vein (say vain) A vein is a tube in the body of a person or animal, which carries blood to the heart.

velvet is a soft material made from cotton, silk or nylon. It has a thick layer of short, cut threads on one side.

vertical Something that is vertical stands or points straight up from a flat surface.

vest A vest is a piece of clothing. People wear a vest on the top half of their body, underneath another piece of clothing such as a shirt.

vet A vet is a person who is specially trained to look after the health of animals. Vet is short for veterinary surgeon.

victory A victory is the winning of a battle or game.

video A video is a machine which can be used to play video tapes on a television set. It can also record television programmes.

view The view from a window or high place is everything that can be seen from there.

village A village is a small group of houses and other buildings in a country area. A village is smaller than a town.

villain
1 A villain is someone who harms other people on purpose, or breaks the law to get what they want.
2 The villain in a play or story is the main bad person in it.

vine
1 A vine is a climbing or trailing plant with long twisting stems.
2 A vine is also a climbing plant which has grapes as its fruit.

vinegar is a sharp-tasting liquid. It is usually made from sour wine or malt. Vinegar is used to add taste to some foods. It is also used for pickling.

violent
1 Something that is violent happens suddenly and with great force: *A violent earthquake shook the city.*
2 Violent weather is very stormy and windy.

violet A violet is a small plant with purple or white flowers.

violin A violin is a musical instrument with four strings. It is held under the chin and played with a bow.

visit
1 If you visit someone, you go and see them.
2 If you visit a place you go and see it: *Do you live here? – No, we're just visiting.*

visor A visor is a movable part of a helmet. It can be pulled down to protect a person's eyes or face.

vitamin A vitamin is something which people need to stay healthy. There are vitamins in many kinds of food.

voice
1 Someone's voice is the sound they make when they speak or sing.
2 If you say something at the top of your voice you say it as loudly as you can.

volcano A volcano is a mountain with a hole called a crater in the top. Sometimes, hot melted rock, gas, steam and ash burst from the crater.

volume
1 A volume is a book.
2 The volume of an object is the amount of space that it takes up.
3 The volume of something such as a radio or television is the amount of sound that it is making: *She played her radio at full volume.*

vowel In the English language the letters a, e, i, o, and u are vowels.

voyage A voyage is a long journey on a ship or in a spacecraft.

vulture A vulture is a large bird which feeds on dead animals. Vultures live in hot countries.

wade To wade means to walk through fairly shallow water.

wafer A wafer is a crisp biscuit.

wage A wage is the amount of money that is paid regularly to someone for work that they do.

wagon
1 A wagon is a strong cart for carrying heavy loads. Wagons are usually pulled by horses or oxen.
2 A wagon is also a railway truck.

waist Your waist is the narrow middle part of your body just below your chest.

waistcoat A waistcoat is a sleeveless piece of clothing with buttons on the front. It fits on the top part of the body. Men often wear waistcoats over their shirts and under their jackets.

wait If you wait, you spend some time before something happens: *Please wait here for a moment.*

wake
1 The wake of a boat is the track of waves that it leaves behind it as it moves through the water.
2 When you wake, you stop sleeping.

walk When you walk you move along by putting one foot in front of the other.

wall
1 A wall is one of the vertical sides of a building or room.
2 A wall can also be used to divide an area of land. This kind of wall is long and narrow. It is built of brick or stone.

wallet A wallet is a small, flat folded case that fits in a pocket. It is used to hold things such as paper money and library tickets.

walrus A walrus is an animal that lives in the sea. It looks like a large seal. It has coarse whiskers and two long tusks. Walruses are found mainly in the Arctic region.

wander When you wander you walk about without planning to go in any particular direction.

want If you want something, you wish for it or need it.

war A war is a period of fighting between countries. Weapons are used and lots of people get killed and injured.

wardrobe A wardrobe is a tall cupboard where you can hang your clothes.

warehouse A warehouse is a large building which is used to store things.

warm (warmer, warmest)
1 Something that is warm has some heat, but not enough to be hot.
2 Clothes and blankets that are warm are made of material such as wool which stops you feeling cold.
3 If you warm part of your body, you put it near something hot so that it stops feeling cold.

warn If you warn someone, you tell them about a danger or problem they might meet.

wash If you wash something, you clean it with soap and water.

washer A washer is a thin flat ring of something such as metal or rubber. It has a hole in the middle. Washers are used to seal or fasten.

washing machine A washing machine is a machine for washing clothes.

wasp A wasp is an insect with wings. It has yellow and black stripes on its body. Wasps can sting.

waste
1 Waste is material that is no longer wanted. This is often because the useful part of it has been taken out.
2 Waste is also the careless use of things such as money or water.
3 If you waste something such as time or money, you use too much of it on something that is not important.

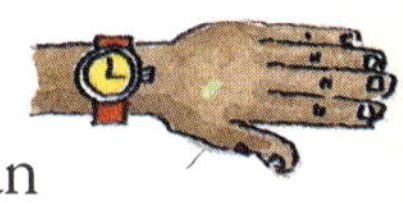

watch
1 A watch is a small clock that you can wear on your wrist.
2 If you watch something, you look at it carefully to see what happens.
3 If someone keeps watch, they look out for danger. This is usually while other people are asleep or resting.

waterfall A waterfall is water that flows over the edge of a cliff to the ground below.

watering can A watering can is a container shaped like a bucket. It has a handle on one side and a spout on the other. A watering can is for watering plants.

waterproof Something which is waterproof does not let water pass through it.

wave

1 A wave is a raised line of water on the surface of the sea or a lake. It is caused by the wind, or by tides making the surface of the water rise and fall.

2 A wave is also a gentle curving shape in someone's hair.

3 If you wave, you move your hand in the air, usually to say goodbye to someone.

4 If something waves, it moves gently up and down or from side to side. For example, flags wave in the wind.

wax

1 Wax is a solid, slightly shiny material made of fat or oil. It is used to make things such as candles and polish. Wax goes soft and melts when it is heated.

2 A special kind of wax is made by bees.

3 Wax is also the yellow sticky material that is found in people's ears.

way

1 A way of doing something is how it can be done.

2 If you say someone is doing something in a particular way, you mean that is how they are doing it: *I don't like the nasty way you said that.*

3 The way to a particular place is the direction you have to go to get there.

4 If someone or something is in your way, they are blocking your path.

5 Way is used to say how far something is: *It's a long way to the shops from here.*

6 If you have your own way, everything happens as you want.

weak (weaker, weakest)

1 People or animals that are weak do not have much strength or energy.

2 If an object or part of an object is weak, it could break easily.

3 Sounds and lights that are weak are very faint.

4 Drinks such as tea or coffee that are weak do not have a strong taste.

wealth is having a lot of money or valuable things.

weapon A weapon is an object such as a gun or missile which is used to hurt or kill people in a fight or war.

wear

1 Wear is the damage or change that is caused by something being used for a long time.

2 When you wear things such as clothes, you have them on your body.

3 When something wears out, it cannot be used any more.

weary (wearier, weariest) If you are weary you are tired.

weasel A weasel is a small wild animal. It looks rather like a long, slim mouse. Male weasels are about 25 cm long from nose to tip of tail. Weasels move very fast. They catch rats, mice and birds for food.

weather The weather is what it is like outside; for example, raining, sunny or windy.

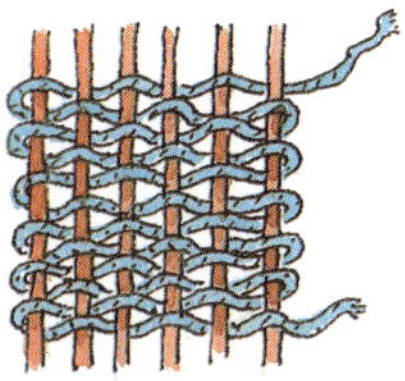

weave
1 When someone weaves cloth, they make it by crossing threads over and under each other. They use a machine called a loom.
2 If you weave something such as a basket, you make it by twisting twigs or cane together.

web
1 A web is a fine net made by a spider to catch flies.
2 A web is also a piece of skin between the toes of water birds. The web helps them to swim well.

Wednesday is one of the seven days of the week. It is the day after Tuesday and before Thursday.

weed A weed is any wild plant that grows where it is not wanted. Weeds grow very strongly and stop the other plants growing properly.

week A week is a period of seven days.

weekend A weekend is Saturday and Sunday.

weigh
1 If something weighs a particular amount, that is how heavy it is.
2 If you weigh something, you use scales to measure how heavy it is.

weight The weight of something is its heaviness. This can be measured in units such as pounds or kilos.

welcome If you welcome someone, you speak to them in a friendly way when they arrive.

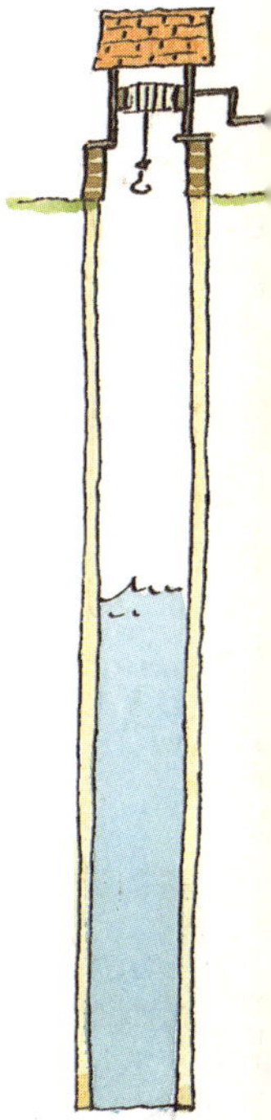

well
1 A well is a deep hole in the ground that has been dug to reach water or oil.
2 If you do something well, you do it to a high standard.
3 If you are well, you are healthy.

wellingtons are long rubber boots that you wear to keep your feet dry.

west is one of the four main compass points. If you face the point where the sun sets, you are looking west.

wet
1 If something is wet, it is covered in water or some other liquid.
2 If the weather is wet, it is raining.
3 If something such as ink or cement is wet, it has not yet dried.

whale A whale is a very large animal that lives in the sea. It looks like a huge fish. Whales breathe through a blow-hole in the top of their head.

wheat is a plant whose seeds are used to make flour. The seeds are called grains.

wheel A wheel is a circular object which turns round on a rod fixed to its centre. Wheels are fitted under things such as cars, bicycles and prams so that they can move along.

wheelbarrow A wheelbarrow is a handcart shaped like an open box. Wheelbarrows usually have one wheel in the front, and two legs and two handles at the back. People such as gardeners and builders use wheelbarrows.

whine
1 To whine means to make a long, high noise, especially one that sounds sad or unpleasant.
2 If someone whines, they talk about something that does not matter very much in a miserable and annoying way.

whip
1 A whip is a thin piece of leather or string fastened to a stiff handle. It is used for hitting.
2 When someone whips cream or egg white, they stir it very fast.

whirlwind A whirlwind is a wind which spins round and round very fast. It moves across the land or sea.

whiskers The whiskers of an animal such as a cat are the long, stiff hairs that grow near its mouth.

whisper When you whisper, you speak very quietly using only your breath.

whistle
1 A whistle is a small metal tube which you blow. It makes a loud noise.
2 When you whistle, you make a loud, high noise. You can do this by using a whistle. Or you can do it by forcing your breath out between your lips.
3 If something whistles past, it makes a loud, high sound as it moves quickly through the air.

whole
1 The whole of something is all of it.
2 If you swallow something whole, you do not chew it.

wicked Someone or something that is wicked is very bad.

wide (wider, widest)
1 Something that is wide measures a large distance from one side to the other.
2 If you open something wide, you open it as far as it will go.
3 You use wide when you are talking about how much something measures from one side to the other: *How wide is this doorway?*

width
1 The width of something is the distance it measures from side to side.
2 A width is the distance from one side of a swimming pool to the other.

wig A wig is a head covering made of hair. People wear wigs because they are bald, or because they want to cover their own hair.

wild (wilder, wildest)
1 Animals and birds that are wild live naturally. They are not kept by people as pets or farm animals.
2 Wild plants grow naturally and are not specially grown by people as crops.
3 If the sea or the weather is wild, it is very strong and rough.

wildlife is animals and other things that live in the wild.

willing
1 If someone is willing to do something, they do not mind doing it.
2 A willing person is someone who does things cheerfully.

willow A willow is a tree. There are many different kinds of willow. Most of them like to grow where it is damp.

win
1 If you win when you are taking part in something such as a race or a game, you do better than the others taking part.
2 If you win something such as a prize or a medal, it is given to you because you have done something very well.

wind (as in tinned) A wind is a current of air that moves across the earth's surface.

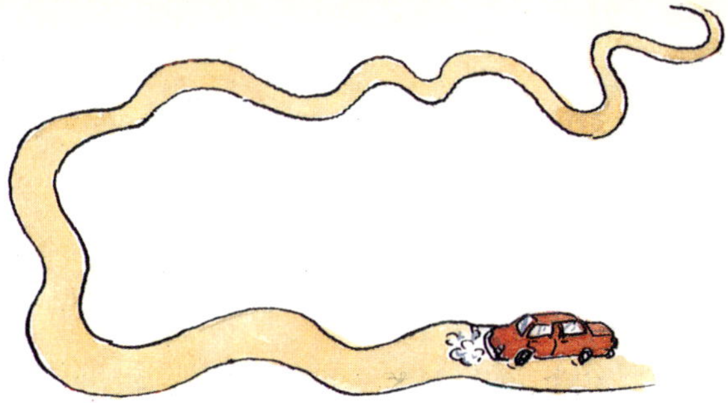

wind (as in mind)
1 If something such as a road or river winds, it has lots of bends in it.
2 When you wind something round something else, you wrap it round several times.
3 When you wind something such as a clock, you turn a knob, key or handle round and round to make it work.

windmill A windmill is a building with large sails on the outside. The sails turn as the wind blows. This makes a machine work inside the mill. The machine crushes corn or wheat to make flour.

window A window is a space in a wall or vehicle. It has glass in it so that light can come in, and you can see through.

wing
1 The wings of a bird or insect are the two limbs on its body that it uses for flying.
2 The wings of an aeroplane are the long flat parts sticking out of its side. They keep the aeroplane in the air.

wink When you wink, you close one eye for a moment. This is usually a signal to someone that something is a joke or a secret.

winter is the season between autumn and spring. In the winter the weather is usually colder than during the other seasons. Many trees and plants lose their leaves.

wipe If you wipe something, you rub its surface lightly with something such as a cloth. This is usually to remove dirt or liquid.

wire is long thin metal. Wire is used for fastening things, and for making things such as bird cages or baskets. Wire can also carry electric current.

wise (wiser, wisest) Someone who is wise is sensible.

wish If you wish that something would happen, you would very much like it to happen.

wobble If someone or something wobbles, they make small movements from side to side: *I wobbled and nearly fell off my bicycle.*

wolf A wolf is a wild animal that looks like a large dog. Wolves live in a group called a pack. They usually live in forests.

woman A woman is an adult female human being.

wonder
1 Wonder is a feeling of great surprise, usually at something marvellous.
2 If you wonder about something, you think about it and wish you knew more about it.
3 If you wonder what to do about something, you are not sure what to do about it.

wonderful If you say something is wonderful, you mean it makes you feel very happy.

wood
1 Wood is material from the trunks of trees. It can be used to make things such as furniture.
2 A wood is a large area of trees growing near each other.

wooden An object that is wooden is made of wood.

woodpecker A woodpecker is a bird with a long, sharp beak. It makes holes in the trunks of trees so that it can eat the insects which live there.

wool is the hair that grows on sheep and on some other animals. Wool can be knitted or woven into material that is used to make things such as clothes.

woollen clothes or materials are made from wool, or from wool mixed with other fibres.

work
1 People who work have a job which they are paid to do.
2 When you work, you spend time and energy doing something which is useful.
3 If something works, it does what it is supposed to do.

world The world is the planet we live on.

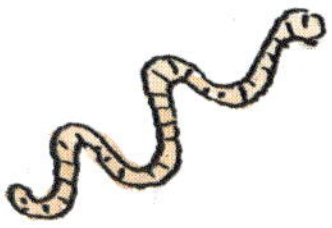

worm A worm is a small animal with a long, thin, hairless body. Worms have no bones and no legs. They live in the soil.

worry If you worry, you keep thinking about problems, or about unpleasant things that might happen.

worship When people worship, they show love and admiration for their god or gods in some way; for example by praying or singing hymns.

worth
1 If something is worth a particular amount of money, it could be sold for that amount.
2 If someone says that something is worth doing, they mean it is enjoyable or useful.

wound (say woond) A wound is a cut or a hole in someone's flesh, usually caused by a weapon.

wrap When you wrap something, you cover it tightly with something such as paper or plastic.

wreck
1 A wreck is a plane, car or other vehicle which has been very badly damaged in an accident.
2 A wreck is also a ship which has sunk or been destroyed at sea.
3 If someone or something wrecks something, they destroy it completely.

wren A wren is a very small brown bird. It is one of the smallest birds in Britain.

wrestle When people wrestle, they fight. They use special holds to try and force each other to the ground.

wriggle When a person or animal wriggles, they twist and turn their body with quick movements.

wrist Your wrist is the part of your body between your hand and your arm. It bends when you move your hand.

write When you write, you use something such as a pen or pencil to make words, letters or numbers.

writing
1 Writing is something that has been written or printed: *She could see some writing on the piece of paper.*
2 Your writing is the way that you write with a pen or pencil: *Julia has very nice writing.*

wrong
1 Something that is wrong is not correct.
2 If a person does something wrong, they do something bad.
3 The wrong side of a piece of cloth or knitting is the side which faces inwards.

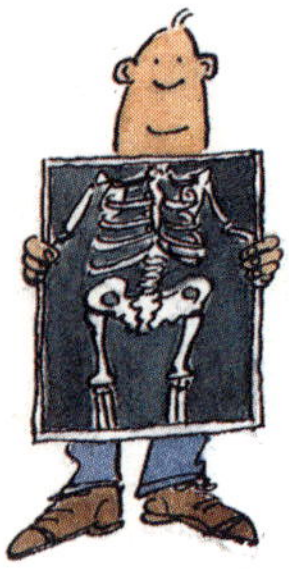

X-ray An X-ray is a ray that can pass through some solid materials. X-rays are used by doctors to examine bones or organs inside people's bodies.

xylophone (say zylofone) A xylophone is a musical instrument. It is made of wooden bars of different lengths which are arranged in a row. You play a xylophone by hitting the bars with special hammers. Each bar makes a different sound.

yacht (say yot) A yacht is a large boat with sails or a motor. Yachts are used for racing or for pleasure trips.

yard
1 A yard is a flat area of concrete or stone, usually next to a building. A yard often has a wall round it.
2 A yard is also a large area where a particular kind of work is done, or where vehicles deliver and collect things. For example, a builders' yard or a timber yard.

yarn is thread, made from something such as wool or cotton. It is used for knitting or making cloth.

yawn When you yawn, you open your mouth very wide and breathe in more air than usual. People usually yawn when they are tired or bored.

year A year is a period of time. It is equal to 12 months, or 52 weeks, or 365 days.

yell If you yell, you shout loudly. People sometimes yell if they are excited, angry or in pain.

yelp If people or animals yelp, they give a sudden, short cry. This is often because they are frightened or in pain.

yesterday means the day before today.

yet You say yet when something has not happened up to now: *She has not come yet.*

yew A yew is a tree that has dark green, thin leaves on its branches all the year round. Some yew trees have red berries. Yew trees grow very slowly and can live to a great age.

yoghurt is a slightly sour, thick liquid which is made from milk.

yolk (say yoke) A yolk is the yellow part in the middle of an egg.

young A young person, animal or plant has not been alive for very long.

zebra A zebra is an African wild animal. It looks rather like a horse with black and white stripes on its body. Zebras live in large herds.

zero is the number 0.

zigzag A zigzag is a line which keeps changing direction sharply.

zip A zip is a fastener used on clothes, bags and other things. It has two rows of teeth which are pulled together with a sliding catch.

zoo A zoo is a park where wild animals are kept so that people can look at them or study them.